JASPER OWENS

Trojumanna Saga

"The Greeks made war on Troy not for the sake of a woman, but because of divine will."

- EURIPIDES

Contents

Preface

I am pleased to present **"Trojumanna Saga"** in its entirety, in English.

This work is based in great part on a supposed first-hand account as found in the Dares Phrygius version, which provides a unique and intriguing perspective on the legendary conflict. It was likely passed down orally before being written in Old Norse.

Unlike other adaptations of the Trojan War, this saga is not an adaptation of the Iliad. Rather, it is a completely different retelling of the story, with its own characters, plot twists, and interpretations of the events that took place. One of the most interesting departures from traditional portrayals of the gods in the story is the replacement of Zeus with Thor, and Apollo being referred to as the Solar God.

Through the pages of this book, readers will be transported to a world of heroic warriors, cunning leaders, and epic battles. They will witness the rise and fall of great heroes, the sacrifices made in the name of honor and glory, and the devastating impact of war on those caught in its midst.

"Trojumanna Saga" is a captivating and thought-provoking tale of the Trojan War that challenges our assumptions about the characters and events of this timeless legend.

I hope that readers will enjoy this unique journey through one of the greatest stories of all time.

In the prologue of Snorri's Prose Edda, we have the following passage:

> *"Thus it is said that when that man of great knowledge, Snorri Sturluson, came to write this book he decided to call it the Prose Edda. He made this book to provide a brief summary of the poems of the Elder Edda, together with explanations of difficult words and stories.* **He said that Asgard was once called Troy, and was situated at the middle of the world."**

In Gylfaginning, chapter 5 of the Prose Edda, it is said:

> *"Þá er þat talat, at menn kölluðu Ásgarð Troja, ok aðrir höfðu þar önnur nöfn"*

> **"Then it was said that men called Asgard "Troy," and others had other names for it."**

1

Jason, Son of King Pallas

Here begins the saga of the men of Troy.

Pallas was a malevolent and cunning king who ruled over a great part of Greece. He was deceitful, but still mighty and powerful. He was father to a son named Jason. (Other sources name Jason as his nephew.)

Strong and well-regarded, Jason earned the people's respect and loyalty. Many wanted Jason to receive his own kingdom from a portion of his father's. So beloved by all the people who knew him, they wanted to give him their obedience, and they held that he would be a very great leader when he separated from other rulers.

Fearful that his son would usurp his throne, Pallas plotted to have Jason murdered. When this proved both challenging and difficult to bear, he assigned Jason a perilous task instead: to retrieve the golden fleece from Colchis.

Pallas said to Jason:

"It is well known to many people that the great leaders who have been in the world have placed their greatest skill and silence in performing great and magnificent deeds so that they might leave behind an immortal name and kingdom. Now it is obvious to people that they have achieved great maturity, strength, and age.

"So if you desire to achieve some fame, then your reputation will spread more than others who are contemporary to you, and I know of no feat that seems more honorable to the young than to seek out the place called Colchis to obtain the treasure that is spun from gold. And this journey will be accomplished with many difficulties from many on the way.

"But your gifts, wisdom, and great strength will lay all human troubles to rest, and yet others might travel there with even greater determination, as it will be most beneficial to them for all time. Now if you want to undertake this journey, I shall give you as much travel equipment as you yourself want."

To build a ship, which he was to steer on this journey, was no small task, but the king commissioned it be done, and the king had the ship prepared with the greatest skill, by the best shipbuilder. It was all built with gold from the keel. Jason sent word to the leaders and told them what he had in mind and asked them to come to his meeting.

All of them promised to follow him, each as long as their life lasts, and promised that when he was ready, he would set sail with his companions. These men prepared themselves for the journey with him, a crew comprising the bravest and most illustrious heroes of the age.

There was Hercules, the strong and the far-famed. He has almost traveled around the entire world and was called the greatest hero in his time, and though peace is not found with him, he rises. He was of such strength that he broke apart two snakes, one with each hand when he was just a young child.

In this journey, Castor and Pollux, the brothers of Helena, who was the fairest of all women of Greece, rose from Spain.

With him also traveled Njástor, the wise man from Pylos, Thelamon from Salamis, and Peleus from Phthia. There were many other men who were said to be destined to travel with Jason.

They named the ship, the most magnificent of all ships, "Argo" after its builder and commenced their voyage. The journey was calamitous for both men and the arms they carried on the ship.

When they reached a place, then they left the harbors. They had come to the land that is called Phrygia, in the harbor that is called Symomenta and went a little ways from the ships to entertain themselves and see the country's customs.

King Laomídón of Phrygia had a son with his queen named Priam.

Priam and his wife Hecuba had five sons. They were Hector, Alexander, Helenus, Delphebus, and Troilus. Their three daughters were Andromache, Cassandra, and Polyxena. Priam also had illegitimate sons who are not named here. While he was alive, King Laomídón had more power over the high-kingdom than Priam did.

When Jason and Hercules arrived at this place, which was already famous in reputation, the locals grew cautious. King Laomídón convened with his men and the other rulers to deliberate on the matter.

Laomídón said to them, "Now they have come from Greece, and you well know that they are courteous and noble men, very noble indeed. When they saw our good land provisions they came with but little preparation. I think that we can expect more troops from Greece in a very short time.

"Now it is my advice, if it seems to you all, that we send them a message to leave our kingdom with good terms if they would do so. It is then my advice that we make terms with them and surrender treasures to them, and let them not stay here any longer with their small army in the land."

All thought this was wise, and so it was done, that men were sent to meet with Jason and told him the king's words that he should depart.

Nothing is told of their journey from there, but they came to Colchis, where a king ruled, named Nesta.

His daughter, Medala, was very beautiful. In the country, there was a great temple, and in the temple, there was a dragon that always slept.

For our tale, you should not be concerned with what was unfamiliar, but that the king and his officials would have it so that the golden fleece could not be taken unless the dragon was killed, and victory be won over the fire-breathing monster, and the golden fleece was in the temple in the dragon's cask. It was too much for most men to go there, as for others it had happened before to end only in misfortune.

Now the king's daughter was told that Jason had anchored his ship at a place called Päfa near Colchis, with such a magnificent appearance that people thought they had never seen such a sight before, and the women urged her to go and meet the sailors and ask for news from where they had come, or where they wanted to go, or whether they were peaceful or not.

Then the king's daughter prepared carefully and went to meet the Greek, and she asked him about his expedition. She thought Jason was the most handsome and dignified of all men in his appearance. Then they began talking to each other, got along well, fell in love, and quickly made their own plans together.

It is from them and all these deeds that we begin our long story.

2

Jason's Fate and Hercules Dishonored

It so happened that Jason reached the cape with bravery and valor. With the advice of the princess and her knowledge, Jason settled there and gained great power and titles, and never returned to Greece.

But Hercules went home to Greece with most of their ancient treasures, and when Hercules returned, he was unhappy with his journey and with the injustice that he thought King Laomídón had done to him. Hercules was on his way home to find Castor and Pollux, who were then thought to be involved in this matter.

It was told in ancient books that they had a mother named Leda, but not the same father for both.

Tébaris was the father of Castor. Hercules went then to Sparta and was well received there.

After that, he found the brothers and asked them how they were with King Laomídón, who had unjustly driven innocent people from his land. He addressed them with great authority and asked if they would not take revenge on the treacherous foreigners.

He said that each should prove his own courage by attacking them with his own hands. The brothers quickly agreed, fully accepting it.

Hercules would rather be their kinsman. He thanked them for their words, for he then planned to find Thelamon of Ætólíá and asked how he would be inclined to seek revenge on King Laomídón for his disrespect.

Thelamon answered, "I am completely eager to go on this journey with you whenever you wish, and contribute all that I can."

After that, Hercules journeyed to Pólans, where the wise Njástor ruled and welcomed him with honor. Hercules said he was aggrieved by the disrespect that King Laomídón had shown them and called on his courage to take revenge if he could.

Njástor highly praised his decision-making, and told him how he ended up worsening relations, over limited matters, with his kin. He then declared Hercules his ally, agreeing to journey with him as requested.

Then, when Hercules had found all those he considered most important and who had promised him their support. He prepared nineteen magnificent and fully-equipped ships for the journey. He chose men who were brave in battle and skilled in combat for this expedition.

He organized everything grandly and well for the journey. Then he sent instructions to all the warriors who were to accompany him on the journey.

When they all arrived at the ships that were to set sail, he provided them with sturdy oars and ensured that they were ready, then set sail, not stopping until they reached the Phrygian harbor called Erges.

3

Hercules Makes War on Troy

She, Troy, was then not strong enough to work for protecting the multitude of people, but there were many bold men there to defend it. When the king was certain that the ships of war had come to land, he rode out with all his host to meet those who guarded the ships.

King Laomídón led his army to confront them. There was a hard spreading there, for there was an intense fighting around the sea-carriages. Then men came running out of the city and said that Hercules had attacked the city itself, so the king wanted leave that fight to go the side of the citizens.

When Hercules had arrived from the ships to the city, he spoke to his men:

"Valiant comrades, you are well aware of our destined path. We must now cast off any timidity that may linger and emerge emboldened, unyielding to the scheming of our adversaries. Nevertheless, we lack the privilege to tarry here indefinitely, waiting for the lord of this land to extend his audience to us.

"Hence, let us brace ourselves to be resolute and dauntless, swift-witted and sagacious. We shall make it unequivocally clear what awaits those who dare oppose us. My intent is to seize the city and its opulent treasures, bringing

"

down King Laomídón as retribution for the affront to our honor.

"This city has known no conquest, be it by the few or the many, despite its modest size. To highlight our resolve in conquering it, I propose selecting our finest warriors to assail from the vantage point closest to its pinnacle, securing the covetable grounds for our foothold. This triumph will attract eager souls seeking glory and a better fate."

He strategically selected the optimal section of the city to initiate the attack, ensuring greater glory and rewards. With this decision, the mission was set in motion.

Now a good rumor was made about his words. They went to the city with much unrest and noise. They encouraged each other to success. Then they attacked the city with much recklessness, but the city dwellers were brave. However, little counsel was there for them because the king, Laomídón, was gone with his highest ranking and strongest wild men.

King Laomídón afterward approached the city and intended to bring comfort to the citizens. Hercules came against him right outside the city with a great part of his army and cunningly fought with strong attack and unbreakable defense. Hercules went so hard forward that he struck with both hands and didn't let go of his weapons until he defeated King Laomídón, and then most of his army followed in death.

Though the city's inhabitants had been courageous, they lacked their leader for most of the fight, as King Laomídón and his elite warriors had departed to meet the Greek ships.

Hercules managed to vanquish King Laomídón and his forces, and he and his men raided the city laden with riches, gaining all its wealth.

Their journey was heard of far and wide throughout the world, and they now enjoyed their portion well. Hercules asked Thelamon what he would most like to choose from the loot, and he chose Eseone, fair daughter of King Laomídón. Hercules greatly agreed to his decision. He was given the maiden with the blessing of Hercules, and they fell deeply in love and then went to Salamis.

The Greeks thought they had now avenged their humiliation and so treated them well as they stood with them.

4

Priam's Inheritance and Antenor's Mission

Priam, King Laomídón's son, was absent during the battle, but upon hearing of the events, he was distraught. He relocated to Troy with his family and all his possessions, where he was crowned king over Laomídón's lands.

Upon arriving in Troy, Priam fortified the city with walls, towers, and other defenses, ensuring the ramparts were secure against potential attacks. He had castles built over each city rampart for the well-being and protection of everything, and the men were well prepared to guard those ramparts and castles.

These were the main fortifications of the city, and they could not be breached even if there were hidden weaknesses.

The formidable strength of the cities of Ótenandi, Danandi, Ilía or Ilion, called also Troy, Seda, Tobría, and Totacta impressed everyone, and they were all completely fortified and so strong that no men thought they had seen such a powerful defense and protection of all parts.

Then he secretly brought additional supplies and provisions under his command, so much that it seemed to everyone as if they would keep all the manpower available every day, and have an excess of all things.

Priam had a great hall built in the city and dedicated it to Thor, and he had great feasts there for the strengthening and encouragement of all his men.

When all things were prepared as Priam wanted them to be, and he had said four things, he sent word to that man who is called Antenor. A Phrygian chieftain, Antenor was a wise, affluent man gifted in diplomacy and possessed a brave and masculine disposition.

Priam requested that Antenor journey to Greece and negotiate peace with the Greeks, asking them to depart peacefully. He cautioned that if they declined, he would not let the issue lie and would pursue a course other than peacemaking.

Priam told him, "You must strive for them to return home," he said. "And I will be very pleased if my sister Eseone can obtain all the peace terms with the Greeks if they accept this proposal, and be returned home. If you could take this message, and if they do not allow this, say that I will not let this matter sit for long, and for this reason, the Greeks will come to understand that the Trojans have other ways than seeking peace if they do not want to heed the requests that I now speak of in this matter."

Antenor replied, "I am willing to further your message as you wish, but as for what I have in mind, the Greeks will not send your sister back, no matter how many demands you make."

Antenor now prepared for his journey, bringing with him good provisions, and he made his way to the meeting in Fliström with Polonius, where he spent the winter in good circumstances.

When that time had passed from Polonius, Antenor sent him a message. He said, "I am an envoy of King Priam, and I have come with this message to seek reconciliation with you. He extends his hand."

He continued, declaring, "You are well aware of the extent to which he must atone for the wrongs you have committed against him. That is, murdering his father, demolishing his stronghold, raiding Phrygia, killing numerous people, and abducting his sister Eseone, his greatest grief. He requests that you play a role in returning her home."

Polonius took his words to heart and admitted that they had not treated him with the respect he deserved, apologizing. They urged him to depart promptly, claiming it was not his doing that King Priam's sister was taken. So Antenor set sail and arrived at Salamis. The sons of Thelamon, Ajax, and Tentór were there. He went to meet Thelamon and asked him to send home to Phrygia the sister of King Priam.

He suggested that doing so could bring about peace between the parties, but Thelamon replied that, "I do not know how to guide you. I have not done worse to Priam than was possible for the sake of his father. I did not kill King Laomídón and I did not steal away the sister of Priam, I proceeded with such valor as was from my hand, I took these rewards for my own deeds, which I promise I will not let them slip away from me."

Having given his response, Thelamon requested that Antenor leave his territory quickly as if he had no other purpose.

Ajax and Tentór, both robust and valiant men, were prepared to make him leave.

Thelamon and Eseone raised their sons in Salamis, where they participated in all the sports and activities that men could engage in. The two were deeply devoted to each other, and in any peril, they would stand united.

When the time for Troy came later, Thelamon's sons left with the finest servants and armor. If one of them fell, neither would return, this was their pact.

Ajax would perish in that war, but Tentór would never come back because he wished to explore the world, and had received no confirmation, so he went to inquire of the gods where he learned this: His own rule which would be, and they answered from Apollo that he should make another Salamis, a new Salamis, and build there, and so he did.

Antenor left there and continued on his quest for peace, arriving at Sparta to visit the home of Castor and Pollux.

They refused to make peace, asserting that no wrongs had been committed. They said that Laomídón the King had done it to himself and his men, a reproach that no worthy man would bear. They said that everything should stand as it had come and asked him to leave as soon as possible.

Antenor then went to the Poles and carried his message to Njástor the wise, telling him how great the danger would be if an agreement could not be reached.

Njástor took his words seriously and said that it was necessary to search for those things for peace which they had spoken upon. Yet, they had little choice themselves. Njástor saw him as most honorable, and asked him to hasten his journey away so no harm was done to him.

5

Antenor Meets Hercules

Then Antenor went from there until he came to Palcedóníu, and there was Hercules "The Strong" who had been the leader in the army of the Greeks when they waged war in Phrygia.

Hercules was the strongest of all men, and among the giants of his race he was the greatest. He was both tall and broad of shoulder and thick of hand, he had long and thick arms and strong and great hands and well-grown with soft fingers, he was fair of hair and had red-brown beard.

He was both handsome and ugly, somewhat, and largely scarred in the face. He was the best of men, generous and kind-hearted, and spoke quickly and fluently. He was so strong that few men could match him in his time, and he was brave and daring in all human endeavors. He either sought victory or death. He had defeated many wild beasts and dragons. It seemed he ever only wanted to have victory or death.

It is said that he fought against the warrior named Eirrepo, who often fell to the ground in that fight. However, with each fall he became even more powerful when he stood up, but he fell again and grabbed himself so tightly that he lost his life.

He also fought a great dragon, which was so fierce that when Hercules struck off one of its heads, two more grew back in its place. But with his bravery, he managed to cut off all its heads at once. Hercules' part in the story ends there, as he went to Africa and performed many heroic deeds, while the Greeks captured the city of Troy. There is a long tale about him, though little is said of him here.

Antenor now takes up his mission and speaks:

"King Priam of Phrygia sent me here for this mission, to ask for what you should expect, that you send home to his sister Eseone with such pleasure as would be bearable. You would be very wise to have a good share in making this agreement with him successful.

"You have nothing to gain by such an outrage as you have committed against him, and now that you want to show him misfortune, it is not in his favor. He asked me to make it known to you that he has the courage and strength to seek his own rights rather than wait for redress for such an insult."

Hercules told him to go home and tell King Priam he did not fear his threats, and he should make more peaceful journeys from now on.

Then he seized Antenor with his strength, face to face he said to him, "That's how it is."

Antenor disappeared in an instant and did not stop in his journey until he reached King Priam's lands.

6

Antenor Returns to King Priam

Upon Antenor's arriving at King Priam's court, the king inquired about the outcome of his mission.

Antenor reported that he had done his utmost to safeguard the king and his people, and to secure honor, respect, and reparations from the Greek army. He then encouraged the king and his people to display courage and engage in battle against the Greeks to avenge their dishonor.

He said, "I have driven you out of danger as best I can and found those men who have the most influence on it, and offered them to take on honor, righteous ways of warfare, respect, and reparations. Now I call upon you to be brave men, for we should avenge your dishonor, and I advise you to show the Greek army your great strength and to diminish them."

King Priam was then very angry with this response.

King Priam called upon his sons and friends, who were his best advisors and greatest friends, to discuss Antenor's proposition. King Priam then spoke and said that he had sent Antenor to Greece to seek peace and retrieve Eseone, and then told of the answer he had been given, and devised to send a final envoy before going to war.

The king said, "To know if any battle might befall us, I would wish that one of my trusted sons be made leader of this journey."

"I would like to say that I could best undertake a thousand tasks and all that was commanded. I would like to add that I could lead the best thousand men that we have." said Hector, the eldest of Priam's shield-bearing sons.

He volunteered to spearhead the expedition to Greece if there could be any honor gained from it. He was prepared to undertake any challenge to avenge the dishonor inflicted upon King Laomídón, but he was also cautious of the Greeks.

Hector said:

"As for myself, I am also keen to attack the Greeks, to make them suffer as we have suffered. But I fear that if we do so, we may suffer in turn. They have put a shield over their weaknesses, and they belong to whoever possesses them. They have many full-time men who are wise and brave, who are quick in battle and skilled in warfare.

"But we are unaccustomed and unprepared for war, and thus unlikely to succeed. The last time we engaged the Greeks in battle was when my grandfather, Laomídón, wished to wage war against them. I fear that the longer we wait, the greater our loss will be. I would live out my days as intended for me, as a humble scholar, but I would not turn away from this mission."

Alexander then stepped forward, stating his willingness to lead the mission:

"I am not afraid to undertake this journey, which our father desires to have done, and it will be to us both for victory and honor. It seems to me no other counsel better than to order this journey in the best way, both by sea and land. It seems to me not to be a voyage of hazard, whatsoever befalls for correction.

Let you see what shift they have made of us.

"Therefore I know that they would expect to go on journeys for their own reasons to seek their portion, and that we should enjoy our share from the partition, as we have had due to our part in it, I would like to be the leader of this journey, it comes to me as a surprise that I go there without errand, for I have dreamt when I was in Daskógi, in the main temple of Apollo, and it urges me greatly to this journey, I think that those moments will now come to me and that what was said before to the Greeks will be made right by my hand. I am urged to undertake this journey, for I have received wisdom from the gods, and what they promise will always be kept, so it will all go as planned. I think the one who travels is more famous than the one who sits at home."

Priam understood his words well, and he said that the gods will make them complete. He asked to be seen clearly and told the fate of their expedition.

Delphébus, another of King Priam's sons, then spoke up and said quickly, but with this thought in mind: I think it is better for us to seek reconciliation and I intend that we will get there without having given the Aesir themselves up.

He said, "I urge you to seek reconciliation, as it may lead to honor for both sides, or else we will inflict some harm on them to increase our honor from what it is now"

After that, Helenus, the fourth son of King Priam, stepped forward and said:

"My mind is different from my brother Alexander. I believe that it would be better to go without any incident, but it is not easy too do so if Alexander takes away the woman who is considered the most beautiful and courteous in Greece. The Greeks will not tolerate it, and we will find that we have neither the power nor the strength to face their anger and hostility. Therefore, I fear that we will lose our friends and family, and this will not lead to any honor for us."

Troilus, the youngest son of King Priam, then spoke up, "I must not waver, although my brother Helenus does this. It seems to me necessary not to stay here merely at the hands of the Greeks, and we must take revenge on them for their betrayals that they have done to us. It seems to me wise to carry out this journey as best and clearly as possible."

King Priam sent Alexander and Delphébus to gather troops. King Priam then addressed the people, speaking of the offenses of the Greeks that they had done to them, and then what Antenor had reported, that the Greeks would not pay for their dishonorable acts.

Priam stated:

"I therefore intend to send an envoy to them, and Alexander my son is chosen as the leader of this force. He will then return, desiring that he should go on a mission of revenge against our enemies, and it is his duty to follow it through. Therefore the respect and honor for us will continue to grow. They should take my friends against me and the highest honor is to follow and obey my will. If anyone speaks against my plans, then let him say it now, and do not complain about what might come later, it will be unnecessary for them to remain silent now."

A man named Pantus, son of a man named Evfiobus, stood up and spoke:

"The man who values wickedness above justice will suffer in the end. My father said that if Alexander were to take a woman from Greece, it would only add to the already great troubles of the world. He considered it more noble to live with dignity than to die in battle against those who seek envy and foolishness."

King Priam rebuked his words and suggestions and stated that nothing would come of such defeatist talk. He said that there were four worthy advisors who spoke against Pantus' counsel. The time had come to prepare for the journey according to the king's will, and the servant was then dismissed.

King Priam then appointed the necessary provisions for the journey, acquiring everything needed for travel, including ships, provisions, weapons, and all the necessary equipment for the journey. Hector gathered an army in Upper Phrygia, where he was born, while Alexander and Delphébus gathered an army in Pream.

Priam's daughter, Cassandra, was skilled in prophecy and foresight, and used her gift to see this journey.

She tried to tell them that, "We are offered to spare Troy and the life of my father and my brothers and all our people, to have respect and comfort."

Not one person paid attention to her words or story. They ran with swift ships and with all that they had. Alexander was the leader of the journey along with Delphébus his brother, Aeneas his cousin, and Polidamantis.

When they were all ready for their journey, they proceeded on their way.

King Priam said that they should make peace with the Greeks if they could return home with the freed Eseone, Priam's sister, and said, "but if this is not possible then they should send me men to examine their strength, then I will come to them with all the strength I can."

They set sail.

7

Alexander's Quest

According to what Alexander said had appeared to him in Daskógi, he seemed to have full belief that no equal woman could be found in the whole world but there in Greece, and he knew her.

Helena, who was the star of Menelaus, already had some messages between Alexander and her, so there were some affections between the words, and when they were ready for all, they left the harbor with all their troops, and had a man as a guide, a man who had previously traveled with Antenor and was called Pardon.

They had sailed in the sea until they arrived in Barteram where Menelaus was in charge, and at that time he was not at home and had gone to Pylos to find the wise Njástor.

Alexander sent word to Menelaus to request a meeting.

Menelaus commanded him to go to his home and said that the queen, Helena, should remain at their home to provide hospitality and pay for reparations, and said that he should have whatever she wanted to give and present. Alexander gladly accepted this message and found it courteous, so he hesitated with what he had in mind, which was to flee with her.

There was a great feast and great celebration held.

Castor and Pollux had gone to their sister Demostena, and when the oath-takers became aware that a ship captain had arrived at the land, they asked who these people were, where they were from, and what they were planning. People told them that Alexander, son of Priam the King, was there with many people, and that they were sent by the King to Castor and Pollux, and they said they would meet before they turned back on their journey.

It was said that the main place was near the custom, and it was so that Helena went there to arrange the service estate that was to be held there. She was also curious to see the dress of better people who were well-known to the country and were foreigners to her. It was told to her before that they would eventually visit her if they did not meet beforehand.

Now Alexander was told that Helena had gone to the court, he made himself ready quickly and smartly, and went there until he found her.

When they found and saw each other, each thought the other was of great worth to the other, and they then said a few words between them. Afterward, for Helena's sake, many enjoyable and expensive times were carried to the court, and things for the entertainment, and heavily plentiful amusements.

Alexander knew of all these distractions, then went to the court to meet Helena and threw a gold ring at her knee and it was written on with runic letters.

Helena, intrigued by Alexander's actions, picked up the ring and read the inscription out loud, "I swear by the gods that I will marry Alexander and become his queen from that day on."

She blushed deeply when she saw this, and since she could not break the promise she had made, she felt betrayed and called it impossible to keep the promise, thinking on it negatively. Alexander said to her that these words came from the gods, and he would obey them. He also said that the third promise would be broken if she broke the previous two holy promises and that she would receive the third of all if she deviated from this path.

Alexander instructed his men to be ready to leave that same night, and he would signal when it was time to depart. They immediately obeyed him. That night, he gave the sign and they went to the court, abducting Helena in distress along with some other women. They took them to the ship and guarded them there.

The warriors had seized Helena and her belongings, and a fierce battle ensued. Many warriors fell, but Alexander emerged victorious, taking many prisoners and spoils before setting sail and eventually arriving at the harbor called Tenidon.

At Tenidon, King Priam was so distressed by Helena's arrival and that she barely spoke and had little food and sleep. Alexander informed King Priam of what had transpired and explained that Helena needed compassion and support to find comfort among her new people.

King Priam kindly accepted the entire account and assured Alexander that the Greeks would seek to reclaim Helena, but he provided her with kind words, gifts, and sweet pleasantries. Helena was delighted with the goodwill shown to her, and a bond of affection formed between her and the people.

He kindly informed Helena of the good advice he had thought, to go with Alexander his son who was the most beautiful and courteous of all men, and be happy.

Upon seeing Helena, Kassandra was terrified, claiming that Helena's presence would be the source of all destruction and the beginning of a great evil. King Priam, enraged by her words, took her away to the house of four kings.

8

Menelaus Calls for Support

Now is to tell of what happened in Greece, after the incident at the court.

Menelaus and his supporters sought the counsel of Njástor in Sparta. Menelaus then sent word to his brother Agamemnon, urging him to join them.

He had in mind to make a journey from Greece to the Trojans with all the power and army that he could. They then sent a message to the chiefs that they should come there to settle the greatest dispute. His hope was that the navigators would be present and they should come there for consultation.

It was ordered for Achilles "The Strong", Patroclus, Deiphobus, Troilus, Diomedes, and Meriones to join, and it was advised that these all should send their ships to Troy.

They dwelt then in the town that is called after Athena. The arrangement went both quickly and fairly.

Meanwhile, Castor and Pollux, fearing the task of searching for Helena, decided to leave their fate to the gods. They boarded a ship and set sail.

Suddenly, a violent storm arose, and the ship disappeared amidst the tempest. People began to speculate that Castor and Pollux had been taken to the heavens, as they were descendants of the gods. Wise men among the pagans claimed that they had become celestial bodies, and many people believed these claims.

As all the Greek ships arrived at the harbor of Atheiphsis XIV, the captains were accounted for, but the ships themselves were not counted, and the names and origins of many remained unknown.

Once all the Greeks who were destined for the voyage had gathered at the harbor of Athena, King Agamemnon called upon the most noble men. He said:

"In the past and present, to this land, all the men who are gathered here, it will be known that the quarrels and conflicts that King Priam and his relatives have inflicted on us, now you know that there is now such a great army gathered here that we will avenge these injustices, we now have no choice but to do something as great and evil as we wish, because it is now known to all that they must agree to pay the most important matters to be strong and steadfast, beautiful and valiant for success, and there is a general agreement that they should follow them with faith and loyalty. We now take precautions and be wary and attentive, what we have against our enemies and three foes, we shall observe and suggest four courses of action, and have good fortune and a keen eye for all our governance, for our honor and the greatest success, it would please me if it be so for you."

He continued:

"We went on a journey to the gods four times, in search of the fourth omen. We chose three of the most remarkable men: Achilles, Patroclus, and Deiphobus. They were well-prepared for the journey and set off for the place called Pollinis, otherwise known as the Solar God's place. We sought all the omens that would tell us the fate of mankind. When they arrived, the omens said the Greeks would gain victory and conquer Troy in the upper part of the war."

King Priam of Troy wanted to show mercy to the Greeks, and so he sent Njástor, the son of Alkías, to the assembly to negotiate peace between the two sides. Achilles and Njástor traveled together to Athens, but no envoys were sent by King Priam.

The Greeks built up an army of 1200 ships and 93 warships, and then each side prepared their own formidable forces.

9

Descriptions of the Trojans and Greeks

King Priam was a respected man in both appearance and peace-making. He was descended from the greatest lineage, and he was beautiful in the eyes and daring.

Hector was distinguished in speech, white of hair and rough-haired, tough and heroic, and with a tenfold bravery, thoughtful and sharp, gentle and honorable, wise and popular among all his men and the greatest rival in battles.

Delphebus and Helenus were like their father in appearance and nature, Delphebus was skilled in warfare, Helenus was a poet, and a great scholar, popular among all people.

Troilus was both great in stature and defense in appearance, and much stronger than his peers.

Honoring the noble and majestic Alexander, he was white in hair-color and thick-haired, very strong and wise, hair soft and pale, eyes the most beautiful, curved at the feet, well-built and honorable.

Aeneas was a fast traveler and the most eloquent of speakers; brave and generous, both harsh and gentle with his friends, tanned-skin from the outdoors, and hard-featured.

Thenor was there too, tall and handsome, merry, wise and obedient.

Hecuba, the wife of King Priam, was beautiful in her figure, and with a slight limp, yet she still carried herself with a noble air, mild and righteous.

Andromache, wife of Hector, was fair-skinned and tall, slender and beautiful, stately and witty when at table, pleasant and generous.

Kassandra was the wisest of women in wisdom and a great woman in form, red-haired and the best of all women.

Alistene was white-haired, graceful and well-grown, with good and much-longed for hospitality, long fingers and low feet, yet well and gracefully grown, and the best of all women, though she seemed no different, delicate and simple, honorable and noble, and she carried herself with more grace and courtesies than most women.

Agamemnon, king of Greece, was handsome of figure, large and strong of limb, valiant and eloquent; he was reverent to his own and bold in his actions, popular, mild and gentle, equally gracious to all and gracious in all things, and ready for leadership.

His brother Menelaus was of a man of honor, strong and ruddy, handsome of figure and endowed with gentleness, generous in spirit and generous in his gifts, and it seemed to him good both to give and receive, one of the most valiant and wise of men.

Achilles, the strongest of all men, was sharp and deep, great in his chest and so in his thighs, thick in his hands and swift of foot, deep arm-lengths and strong grips, handsome of figure, firm and fair of eye, his hair curled, thick and hard, and the most endured of all locks, gentle and faithful in his eyes, eager and fierce to his enemies, industrious, thrifty and exceeding wise in all his affairs, and the greatest of warriors for bravery and valor.

Patroclus was a strong man, well-joined with great eyes and courageous beyond measure, very big in size yet still young in age.

Ajax, son of Thelamon, was a great and very strong warrior, hardened in battle, brave and skilled in warfare, an expert with weapons, and the best of men - wise and understanding.

Of all the warriors, Diomedes was the strongest; he was noble in his presence, sharp and manly in his conduct, eloquent in his words, swift and expert in all his endeavors.

Protoselaus was strong and noble in his presence, with well-shod feet, an expert with weapons and reliable in his best endeavors.

Njástor was tall and wise, his limbs long and his face graceful. He was wise and the greatest in wisdom.

Nepptholimus "The Great" was wise and majestic in appearance, his speech eloquent. He was kind to his people but hard on his enemies, his limbs long and his eyes bright, handsome and renowned for his courage in battle. When angered, he was the fiercest.

Ulysses "The Strong" was a strong and great man on his journey, submissive yet generous in his deeds, wise and prudent in his counsels, eloquent and thoughtful, and brought money unexpectedly.

Palamedes was a handsome man, hard-waxed and well-disciplined, strong and thoughtful, noble and dreamy. He was honorably praised for his weapons and did not spare his men, peace was his to his and courteous in his gifts.

Machaon was a great man, strong and fine, wise and skilled, patient and merciful to all people.

Mæreon was red-haired, honorable in stature, courteous, wise, patient and hardy.

Castor and Pollux were alike in all things, wise counselors, fair-haired, open-minded, keen-eyed and very tall; they were the brothers of Helena.

Helena's sister was like them in appearance, the fairest of all women, and simple; she was the most beautiful of all women, with a small and fair mouth, between the eyes there was a small spot of down, which could be killed by a finger, and was of gold color, so it seemed to everyone who saw it, except for Ulysses' prophetess Driscida.

Driscida was a tall woman, fair of hair-color and soft of hair, comely of body shape, and her eyes close together and green. She was pleasant in her bearing but seldom looked upon men, and of all women she was the most gentle and simple.

10

Preparing for War

When men prepared to meet Agamemnon king and the others who had intended to leave home and siege Troy, it greatly increased in their eyes the grief of parting from their possessions and kin, distress and poverty.

Protoselaus prepared to go home and took his weapons with him. As he was leaving, he killed someone at his feet. His wife was there and said, "I've never seen you so far away as now, and I fear this might mean even more. You will not come back unless you follow all my advice." He asked her what advice she thought he should follow so he could return.

She said, "It's wise that you killed at the feet, and that you obey my advice. Put your ships in the harbor so they can see each other. When your crew goes ashore, make sure there are a hundred men each. That will be enough. But if you don't take my advice, we'll never see each other again."

So the Greeks prepared to leave the harbor and the sound of weapons clashing filled the air as the ships' benches were lowered from the landings.

Polixenus was their guide, and they landed at a village in the plain of King Priam, called Tenidon. They plundered the cattle and killed the men, there was little to no defense from the countrymen. The Greeks quickly escaped with their spoils and the news was carried to King Priam.

Agamemnon was the king of Greece, and these were the bravest with him, Menelaus his brother, Achilles the strong, Patroclus his father's brother, Palamedes and Diomedes, Ajax, Nepptholimus, Ulysses, and Njástor, they were the wisest masters of Greece.

King Priam's four best warriors were leading the Trojans: Hector, Alexander, Delphebus and Helenus, as well as Troilus, the youngest son of the King.

Hector, the most famous of King Priam's sons, was renowned for his greatness and courage. Aeneas, a great leader, had a wife of the daughter of King Priam named Creusa. Pantarus, Sarpedon, Ascanius, Epistrophus, Menon, Antenor, and Amphimacus were among the great warriors of King Priam. Anchises, Aeneas's father, was already very old and had been a great leader and wise scholar when the Greeks invaded their land.

Agamemnon then sent Diomedes and Ulysses to meet King Priam and ask him to give Helena back to her husband without argument and settle the quarrels, thus ending the attacks and wrongdoings. King Priam took this message heavily and then clearly saw what had passed between them and how harshly he seemed to be held by both his father and his sister Eseone, and also of the plundering and raiding which had been done in his kingdom. King Priam then sent the men back to their husband with this decision and told them that this advice had been held.

While Ulysses were gone, Achilles and Telephus had taken their army to Misia, where they plundered and burned villages. When the news reached King Tevtras, he assembled an army and marched toward Achilles with a huge force. In a great battle, Achilles proved too strong for any of Tevtras's men and they all fled, including Tevtras himself. Achilles then inflicted a grave wound on the king. Telephus intervened and covered Tevtras with a shield in order to save his life. Achilles declared that Telephus must be loyal to Agamemnon and fight their enemies in exchange for his life.

Achilles said, "If you want to stand against our enemies and make great obedience to King Agamemnon, then you should be true and loyal to him in all your service."

Telephus answered, "When I was but a little child, my father Hercules gave a feast to King Tevtras, but then the kingdom went so that the king Diomedes won many deeds and counsels. Then my father Hercules faced him and felled him and freed the kingdom and all the land of Tevtras, and so I wanted to come to the aid of him this time."

Tevtras was grateful, and in thanks for his life, gave Telephus the kingship of Misia and all its lands. Telephus would lead the crafty court of Tevtras and gave him due honor and respect.

Achilles spoke, "Telephus, take this kingdom that you have now obtained and rule it as best you can. Each year, send us men armed with provisions. Your bravest men will see to it. We shall take this opportunity and Telephus shall be in charge of the kingdom. I shall now return to my army and inform Agamemnon, the King, of all that has transpired until this point."

When the messengers returned from the meeting with King Priam, Palamedes arrived with an uncounted number of ships and informed Agamemnon that he had been ill and none of his men had come to his army until that point. Now he would bring them all.

Agamemnon then gathered all the troops and spoke to them, asking them to be united and obedient to those in command. He asked if it would be better to attack the city at night or during the day, and Palamedes agreed to attack during the day.

They believed that would be done in a few days, so all rulers agreed that it should be done on a specific day, which they planned, and then they launched the whole fleet from the harbor, and went until they came to Troy with the whole army.

Priam, who was at the walls with some of his wild men, great warriors, saw the Greek fleet which was massive and quickly descended from the wall's skirts. He called all the chiefs and sent word to the house assembly.

He spoke before the people of the land:

"Now here have come with audacity the Greeks our greatest enemies, and have recently taken land and have a great army, then many uncertain journeys will have gone this far, they are heavily armed, and we will expect hard assaults and sharp battles from the Greek chiefs and their stout ships that steer the army, and yet the almighty will soon be alarmed and unsteady, if they find that there are stronger soldiers before them, and it is my advice that all our army be prepared as soon as possible for battle and go against them, and defend our kingdom, so that they may not land,

"Let them find that there are soldiers here rather than cowards, who now advise them not to look back when they have most reasons to finish, therefore I beg all the dukes and those who are county chiefs, to strengthen and encourage all those men whom each of them has commanded, for assault and victory, then I shall afterward honor each man as he goes boldly in this battle, we may then be called brave men if we drive them off with vigor and avenge our mistreatment, which they have done to us and all our people!"

All the wisest men agreed it was best not to let the Greeks land with their army.

11

The First Two Days

The Trojans sounded their trumpets and prepared for battle, with each knight armed with weapons and boldness. King Priam led his army out of the city, down towards the ships, preparing to defend the Greeks from ascending. The Greeks saw the Trojans in their dress, and King Agamemnon urged his men to attack fiercely.

Both sides raised the battle-cry, and a hard battle ensued with great loss of life. Both sides shot arrows and spears, cast stones, and used any weapon they could find.

The Greeks attacked with shouts and cries, making sure they were arrayed with arrows and swords. Protoselaus attacked the most fiercely on land with his band, and the Trojans followed him in pursuit - many of them falling.

But the Trojans had the greatest champion of their army, Hector, son of King Priam, fighting with them.

Hector saw his men falling and fleeing, so he strode forward and struck with both hands, riding bravely with his sword. He went through the ranks ferociously, so that all retreated until he met Protoselaus, and they had a battle until Protoselaus fell.

The whole troop of Protoselaus fled, and Hector returned to the city while the battle continued.

Achilles asked about the fall of Protoselaus and the deaths of his men, and then came ashore with his own men and many troops. It was the hardest battle, and there was a great cutting of arms when they stood equally on land each against the other. Men fought with troops and riders, and in some places better on both sides.

Achilles pushed so hard that those against him fled, and there was great flight into the Trojans' side. Then night had come, and it became so dark that no more fighting could be done. The Trojans locked the city walls and prepared cautiously, letting the walls protect them in the night.

King Agamemnon was now exhausted, he set his encampments close to the city where there was a great open space and a beautiful plain. They prepared themselves carefully, and erected strong fortifications around their encampments, and dug deep ditches around it.

The next morning, Hector went out of the city with a multitude of people, and King Agamemnon immediately rode against him with the Greek army, and the sharpest war ensued. There was a sharp clash of weapons and swift hearts, each one wanting to avenge their wrongs on the other. More courage was shown in cutting deeply than shielding oneself from great wounds, and many men were quickly killed.

Hector strode forward, fearless and determined, and with one swift stroke he struck down Patroclus, the cousin or uncle, and sworn-brother of Achilles. As Hector moved to strip Patroclus of his clothes as a symbolic act, Mæreon rushed forward to stop him. But Hector proved too strong for him, and quickly overpowered him, seizing the garments he was after.

Menelaus, witnessing this act of disrespect, charged at Hector and struck him in the feet with his sword. The blow took a toll on Hector, weakening him greatly, but he refused to give up. After this wound, Hector was enraged and prepared to slay all in his path.

Hector would have done so, but Ajax, son of Thelamon, then stepped forward to face Hector in battle. The two warriors clashed, their weapons striking sparks as they fought fiercely. For a time, neither was able to gain the upper hand, not a single wound was inflicted.

They both suddenly realized that they were kinsman, closely related. With a newfound sense of kinship and understanding, they ended the battle and exchanged gifts as a symbol of their newfound friendship.

In the aftermath of the battle, the Greeks made a request of the Trojans, asking them permission to erect stones in honor of the fallen soldiers over two years. The Trojans, however, granted ten years to complete this task. The stones were set up and well kept to a certain time, and no one was allowed to disturb those stones that were set.

Agamemnon, the leader of the Greek army, insisted that the Trojans tend to the wounded and bury the fallen soldiers, with the help of the skilled healer Protoselaus.

12

Two Years of Uneasy Peace Ended

After the agreement, Achilles mourned the loss of Patroclus deeply, and Agamemnon hosted a feast for the soldiers, complete with games, songs, and poetry.

During the festivities, Palamedes spoke out, questioning Agamemnon's role as king over the Greek army. He argued that true leadership requires justice and fairness, and that the army should be led by the wise and experienced, and accustomed to battles, not one man. He called for a change in the way the army was governed.

When Palamedes had said what he wanted, they seemed to find that he himself would want to take the position and the name of the noble, so no one took his word, for no one was about any change in the governors, and all was as it had been before.

Two years of uneasy peace passed, and once again war broke out. The Greeks were led by Agamemnon, Achilles, Diomedes, and Menelaus. The Trojans were led by Hector, Aeneas, and Troilus. The battlefield was a chaotic and bloody scene, with both sides fighting ferociously to gain the upper hand.

Hector was a very brave fighter and had four golden shields, and with great courage he defended each of them, and inflicted much damage to the Greeks, and killed many men, leaving a trail of destruction in his wake. He came face to face with Boestes, a powerful duke of a great kingdom.

When they met, each one hurled his weapon against the other. Boestes threw his spear against Hector, but his shield was so strong that the spear did not penetrate it. Hector then thrust his own spear forward, piercing through Boestes' shield and breastplate, and even coming out his back. Boestes died on the ground.

As the battle raged on, Hector continued to fight with fierce determination, facing off against Archilochus in a sword fight and engaging in a duel with Anchinor. Hector defeated Anchinor, who fell dead to the ground. Troilus fought bravely, as did Aeneas, and the Greeks now suffered a heavy defeat in this battle, and the night ended the fight.

Agamemnon addressed his men on this night, and spoke to them, "You know, good chiefs, of these wars which we have had with the Trojans, on us a heavy fall has come, we have lost much people and many of the best lads of our men."

He then bade the dukes to courageously go forward and seek out the life of Hector, he showed them what revenge he should have, and how many chiefs Hector had slain, and said he thought almost all of it undeserved, if he were judged, and he thought he was in the thoughts and hearts and all of honor and courage of all men.

Menelaus,brother of Agamemnon king, stood up and spoke, "It is truly true, lord," said he, "that we two have suffered a great loss of men since we come to Phrygia, many undeserving ones have divided the gold which we had with Alexander, and I think it best that we fight one on one and divide the victory, which of us two shall bear the greater share, then we make our weapons ready, and either I will give my life if we come one on one, or he shall conquer."

These words came before Alexander and he said he was ready to try weapons with Menelaus and one on one, and Helena heard this discourse and knew their counsel, she let Alexander go in that danger to fight with Menelaus but said it was not his fate to go against him, but courage and manhood, and so it shall be avenged, she says, they have borne it together that Alexander shall have nothing except for the eagle, he would have him and be the council of this, on nothing.

All the leaders of both sides were so guests in grief and friendship with each other, who wanted to avenge their own offenses, against their enemies, and now both were to spend the night, and they took care to the night's band.

The next morning, Hector ordered the trumpets to sound, and he led the Trojans out of the city, accompanied by Aeneas and Alexander. They rode towards the Greeks, and the fiercest battle was fought between them with great courage and force.

As the battle raged on, Alexander and Menelaus met in combat, their weapons clashing with deadly precision. Helena watched from the safety of the city walls, her heart heavy with sorrow and distress. She had already lost most in her life, and had been disgraced and carried away. As she watched the battle unfold, she feared that she would soon be led away in disgrace again, a captive of the Greeks.

In the heat of battle, Alexander drew his bow and took aim at Menelaus, his arrow flying true towards the Greek warrior. The outcome of their fierce battle hung in the balance, with both sides fighting with all their might for victory.

When Menelaus had been wounded, he was so enraged that he did not stop until he had killed the horse beneath Alexander and then grabbed the helmet from Alexander's head and tore it off. Menelaus called over Ajax.

Menelaus and Ajax intended to kill Alexander, they intended to stomp him dead, they would have taken him to the underworld if Aeneas had not come to help him with a great band of knights, and Aeneas shot arrows over Alexander, but Hector took him away from their weapons and Aeneas took him, very wounded, home to the city while Hector kept up th fight against Menelaus until night.

Throughout the battle, the line between friend and foe became blurred, and there was a great loss of life on both sides.

Helena seemed to have gone according to her fate and let Alexander fight with such a great man or go in such a way longer, she says Menelaus would be the most horrible to him, and it would not be for innocence for they were to be three. But he did not let himself be divided and seemed to have no time for words of the mother, and fortune, and magnanimity, and said this will be done later.

The next day, the Greeks, led by Achilles and Diomedes, rose up against Hector and Aeneas. The battle was fierce and bloody, with both sides fighting with all their might. Hector felled seven great leaders of the Greeks, while Aeneas took down two. Achilles and Diomedes each claimed four and three leaders of the Trojans, respectively.

As the battle raged on, Agamemnon realized that there was a great loss of men. The Trojans took better care of their soldiers than the Greeks, as Agamemnon struggled to keep his people motivated and urged them to continue the fight. He urged them to the strife and said he would give a heavy penalty if they did not take more into their hands than they had before. It seemed that many had fallen from their suffering and their strength had diminished greatly.

The next day, all the Greeks went out of their quarters to fight and against the Trojans and the conflict was so hard and fierce that it lasted eight grueling days. Each side spared nothing in their efforts to defeat their enemies, and many more lives were lost in the process.

This long battle had been going on for some time, and Agamemnon, the king, said that every day many thousands of his men fell, and there was no hope of burying the dead. He saw that it could not continue this way, so he sent Ulysses and Diomedes to King Priam to ask for peace and weep for three years to heal the wounds and bury the dead, and to revive their quarters and vigor and make weapons, and each could increase their strength as much as possible, and prepare whatever they wanted.

When they arrived at the city, the sun rose and a man named Delon came to meet them and asked if they were carrying weapons at night, and they said they were sent by King Agamemnon and had to go to King Priam to plead for peace. Then they went to King Priam and carried out their mission as they were commanded. Priam asked this of his sons and the other council, and asked whether it should be granted or not as requested.

Hector was the first to speak on this matter:

"It seems strange to me if you let something pass that is requested here, since we have had some quarrels with the Greeks. They have given us the lives of many of their bravest men, and I consider their strength to have departed. They have also asked for peace and we have granted it to them. But now it is my advice that we not give them so long a time of peace, nor any truce, that they can increase their strength to resist us.

"It is difficult for them to improve their rule over distant lands, as they must seek out all the money that can benefit them. But for us Trojans it is more advantageous, for we are within our own land and can here increase our defense strength. And it is my advice that we should not give them this peace for so long, for tomorrow I would have us leave the city with all its own defenses, and make them such a hard attack that they may wish to have never found us."

Despite Hector's reservations, King Priam ultimately decided to grant the Greeks' request for peace after consulting with his other chieftains.

The two sides agreed to a truce of some time, during which time they would work to heal their wounds and strengthen their armies. But as history has shown, peace between the Greeks and Trojans was short-lived, and the war would eventually resume with renewed vigor and intensity.

It is good to say that they so well kept the truce on both sides that whenever they were reconciled, there was no risk to each other even if they met fathers, brothers, or other relatives, and those dead were buried like dead men who had fallen, and the wounded were healed, and then about the walls of Troy and altars and other repairs, and the Greeks let dig many pits and large about their camps and built up against each other as much as possible.

13

Three More Years of Peace - Broken by Battle

Three years had passed since the Trojans and Greeks agreed to a truce. Hector and Aeneas left Troy to face the Greeks, led by King Agamemnon, with Achilles, Diomedes, and Menelaus. The battle was fierce, and many warriors fell on both sides. Hector fought with incredible valor in a terrible conflict against the three great Greek chiefs, Phillip, Anthiphum, and Mæreon. Achilles also contributed to the carnage by killing Lychadonem and Tefforbum from the Trojans.

The fighting continued for thirty days, with many more men falling on both sides. King Priam saw that the divisions and deaths were mounting, so he sent men to King Agamemnon to beg for a six-month truce, which was granted with the advice of his chiefs and friends.

After the truce, a hard battle began, with fourteen armies standing together for twelve days. Again, many great warriors fell from both sides, and there was not enough time to mourn them or tend to the wounded.

Priam agreed to what had been said, but on the next night, when the time of battle was to be, the day after, then Andromache, Hector's wife, had a small dream and told him that he should not go into battle that day and said that he would be wounded if he did not follow her advice.

Hector answered in this way: "There is no trust in the dreams of women and you cannot advise our warfare. With my fate, if the fate has decided that my last days have come, then the battle will surely come, and my life will be as fate wills."

Hector refused to heed her warning, believing that his fate was in the hands of the gods.

Andromache was afraid of his answer and sent word to King Priam, urging him not to let Hector go into battle. King Priam, too, forbade Hector from fighting, fearing the loss of his son. He knew that the Trojans depended on Hector's leadership and strength, and that his death would be a devastating blow to their cause. Priam urged him to stay behind and let others take up arms in his place. Priam the king then commanded his son Helenus to lead with Alexander, Troilus, Aeneas, and Mariones.

Hector became very angry with Andromache for his captivity. He asked to be brought all his armor. He said he would never abide by it, even if by flight he be allowed to follow his brothers to battle.

Andromache then became very scared and threw their young son, who was called Astyanathon, towards Hector and said:

"You take this young son of ours for custody and guardianship, or who will keep him after your life days, or who will avenge you if this your young son is killed or taken captive by the Greeks, or who will strengthen him, or who will help me, or give support to a manless woman, and although you do not want to hear and accept my prayer, then do it for the sake of this boy who is not yet a man, if he could keep you whole, he would soon become a good man."

She wept bitterly and asked him with many beautiful words not to go to battle.

He gave no heed to her words. Andromache went to meet King Priam and asked him to stop Hector from going to battle that day, she told him her dream and all the same of the others. King Priam then spoke to Hector and said he would lay down all his wrath if Hector went to battle that day, and then he sat back down, and not with good behavior, and became very angry.

The Greeks were led by King Agamemnon, Achilles, Diomedes, and Ajax Lothranis that day. Seeing the Trojans without Hector leading them, the Greeks attacked fiercely.

As the battle raged on without Hector, many leaders from both sides fell, but there were more casualties among the Trojans. The noise and shouting from the battle echoed throughout the city as the kings themselves now fought fiercely. Agamemnon, Achilles, Diomedes, and Ajax fought with bravery, but none as brave as should they have fought against Hector.

Agamemnon encouraged his men to fight as bravely as possible, saying that, "We would not get into better circumstances than now when Hector is not to be feared, first he is not in the battle, and they shall now pay for it, let us now avenge our wrongs and remember every injury they have done to us."

The Greeks were now fierce, Achilles had now come forth into the Trojan ranks. He then slew a great chieftain at his left with a spear, so it went out on the other side, and threw him dead to the ground. The Greeks now rallied up their troops, some squads of Trojans were now nearly on the run.

Hector was in a castle with few men which stands in the city, he heard the clamor of their troops and the noise of strife and weapons clash, and it now seemed that the Trojans will suffer heavily.

Hector then jumped up quickly and said: "Get me my shield and my military attire, I cannot bear to know that enemy guards are slaying comrades and sworn brothers, and the very best of warriors, while I lie here like a cat in a nest and get worked into hopeless danger? The enemy guards must come to a fight, and I shall fall with valor before I do not avenge the souls of friends and kinsmen."

Hector threw his armor over himself, it was as hard as steel, both wide and well-fit and shining white as silver. He put a helmet on his head, it was thick and enduring, veiled and clear as glass, he fastened his shield to his side, it was as thick stone and steadfast, then he girded himself with the sword that was the best of all swords.

He said, "It is likely that many Greeks will serve up their lives after this day has passed."

He then took his spear all gold-clad and climbed onto his best horse and rode out to battle.

14

Hector's Final Battle

It was said that his arrival was unexpected when the Aetolians and Greeks came together. As he rode towards the battle he now saw great casualties, and many of the best boys of the Trojans lie dead on the ground, and those who were left were almost fled, and when he arrives he eggs on other men to gather their strength.

"Let us now bravely arm the boys!" he said, "Let us now go forward and take away our enemies and avenge our friends and strengthen our families!"

With his arrival and urging, the Trojans were greatly strengthened, and all his enemies feared him. Hector sought out fiercely anyone who was condemned to death by his weapons. In the first attack, he met a chief named Admeton and struck him with his sword, splitting his helmet in two. He then felled another chief named Phidun with such a blow that he was immediately defeated. Finally, he threw his spear at the chief Albanus, wounding him badly and making him unable to fight.

Now all men, from the honorable men to the dishonorable, feared him. Hector's success had given hope that the Greeks would be much less determined to win Troy if he had kept up the same manner and deeds. Everyone is bound to follow their fate, and no one is so strong as to not be overcome by anyone. Despite this, Hector was still foremost among his men and sought out the greatest deeds.

It was then that Achilles saw what Hector had done.

And he pondered how much people and good warriors Hector had felled from their side, then he would rather quickly serve his life than avenge them not. Now he advanced most valiantly and would gladly meet them bearing the same name. Hector then encounters a great chieftain of the Greeks, who was a duke and named Rolibetus, and when they met, Hector pierced him with a sword and Hector wanted to strip him of his clothes.

In this encounter, the greatest warrior, Achilles, approached him, and when Hector saw him, he turned to face him with utmost dignity. They fought their duel with great blows, and when men saw that these two extraordinary men had come to test their weapon skills, great fear and awe arose among the people.

Hector struck a powerful blow at Achilles, who parried with his shield, but Hector struck again below it, hitting his thigh and then breaking his breastplate, inflicting a severe wound. Achilles became frightened by this wound and attacked much more fiercely than before, causing Hector both pain and injury, but he defended himself with great courage and valor.

In the end, Hector fell dead to the ground with great courage and many severe wounds.

It should be noted here how great and noble a warrior Hector was, for when Achilles killed him, he gained such great fame that his name was praised throughout all foreign lands. The Greeks took Hector's body and carried it to their quarters.

With Hector's fall, a great panic and storm arose among the Trojan ranks, and soon after, they fled to the city while Achilles pursued them all the way to the city's walls, bringing the night of battles.

Then Achilles sadly went back to his quarters, the Greeks were now happy and thankful, and celebrated a beautiful victory, but a great sorrow was over the Trojans, and they wept greatly for the death of Hector.

They thought they had never seen such a hero fall, as when Hector fell, and they thought that no worse thing could happen to them after they had lost him. They wept bitterly, feeling that they had never experienced such a devastating defeat before.

On the fourth day following the battle, the Trojans engaged in a fierce struggle with Menon, resulting in many casualties on both sides. Many were left severely wounded, and Agamemnon, the Greek king, offered reparations for six months for those who lay among the dead and injured. The wounded cried out for help, and Priam, the Trojan king, agreed to the reparations as requested.

15

Priam's Visit, Short Peace-Times, and Achilles in Love

On the first day of the reparations, a truce was called and men were permitted to go about their business freely. It was then that Priam, stripped of his armor and clothing, unarmed and destitute, left the city, and made his way to the quarters of Achilles.

He fell to his knees before Achilles, holding a great gold ring in his hand as a gift, and spoke with great sincerity:

"Achilles, you good warrior and greatest hero and the strongest shield of all Greece, a true Drengr. I offer you all our kingdom and my old age shows me your great courage. Be merciful to me now, gracious in prayer, and accept from me this golden ring and grant me in return the body of my son Hector. And if you bow before either of these, my urgent prayer or the fair beauty of the gift, then I ask that you become my slayer, and may we both have a grave together, for by killing Hector you have defeated King Priam and all the Trojans, but you should become a merciful father to me, and let it come to your mind that you have already won the victory, and various leaders must always rule over them. Now it may be that more needs to be done cunningly, and not everything leans in the same direction, for it is in the power of the gods how it shall go."

And when Priam finished his speech, Achilles took Hector's body and handed it over to King Priam in the manner he himself desired. King Priam went home with the body of his son and it was then carefully buried, and it was made of marble with great and impressive craftsmanship.

Over his tomb, there was a vault and many of his brave deeds were inscribed, which will long be remembered and will not soon be forgotten. It was a great comfort to his surviving relatives, and his tomb was so carefully prepared that his relatives and friends would choose to honor it.

Once this agreement had been reached between the two sides in the battle, Palamedes sought to be appointed king and leader of all the Greek armies. He boasted greatly of his achievements and other successes, speaking a lot about them. Agamemnon, the king and father of the ruler, sought and asked his commanders that they should hold him in charge of the kingdom. Agamemnon then asked his men if it was known to all of them how Palamedes wanted to divide the leaders, or how many terms he would grant me in terms of leadership.

King Agamemnon and his father's rule were disregarded, and all his chiefs were urged to consider him for the kingdom.

King Agamemnon then pleaded with his men, saying:

"It must be well known to all of you what words Palamedes lets be heard about the change of chiefs, or how many accusations he brings against me for lack of control, and calls me incapable of governing or having authority over such a great army gathered here. He also speaks the truth, and now he wants to take on the responsibility of being the leader of all of us and take the king's name. You may make that decision which is in everyone's mind."

Now, as he greatly praised his strength and fortune, it was the decision of the Greeks to accept him as king. He thanked them well with many beautiful words, as they had made him such a great man. He promised some improvements in justice to those who had supported him best for the kingship, saying it was not good to follow such a custom.

"And it will not be long," he says, "before most of you will be as I am."

But even though he spoke like this to them, no such place was prepared. And when the time came to fight, Palamedes led all the Greek forces out of their quarters against the Trojans. He greatly encouraged them to brave advances, saying that each one should take up what he was aiming for and receive such honors from him as each was capable of accepting. It would be tested how well each advanced.

Delphébus and Sarpedon had arrived there. Sarpedon was the first to step forward among the Trojans and fought very courageously, bringing down many valiant men from the Greeks. He met a hero named Néthólimus, a great leader and a brave man. They had a fierce exchange of weapons and inflicted many blows and great injuries on each other.

And so their exchange of weapons ended with Néthólimus falling; both were fierce, and this battle lasted for several days. More men fell on both sides, but more from the Trojans. Then King Priam asked for a truce to go over the sea in a ship for a two-month journey. Polydorus agreed.

At this time, Polydorus sent Agamemnon to Misia for the supplies that Telephus had promised to provide when they needed them. But when Agamemnon came to him, Telephus was displeased with the division of the kingdom they had made and said it would not end well. Agamemnon said it had not been done against his will and claimed he would rather follow the original plan. Polydorus then ordered the ships to be prepared and fortified his camp. King Priam also fortified the walls of the city and its towers.

Polydorus had a trench dug around his camp and prepared in the boldest way possible, and had nine ready all his power, so that everything would be ready when the battle was to be fought again.

When the burial day of Hector came, King Priam, Queen Hecuba, and their daughter Polyxena went to his place, and they had there good service and mourning, as was customary when dignitaries were buried or relatives of powerful men.

Then Achilles went there as they were staying, and he saw Polyxena, the daughter of King Priam, who was the most beautiful and fairest of all the women that men had seen there. Achilles was so captivated by her that he almost forgot the grief he had for Hector, and so love overcame him that he could hardly rise from his seat.

Achilles made such a desire for himself that Polyxena should be his wife to comfort him, but maybe he preferred the honor of King Agamemnon even more. The next night, Achilles sent his confidants to meet Queen Hecuba to ask for Polyxena for his bride, and said he would promise that he would not return home if he married her, and said he would do many other things to the chieftains in the army if Priam granted his request.

Hecuba received Achilles' words well and said she would bring up his case to King Priam and be there to promote the adoption of that advice. Achilles' envoys returned home and told him the end of their mission and how each word had been received.

At that time, Agamemnon returned with great supplies and the good force that Telephus sent to the Greeks.

Hecuba held a discussion with King Priam, touching Achilles' hand, and thought it likely that good would come of it if he refrained from anger, as no one was quicker in the Greek army than him. King Priam pretended he wanted to marry his daughter to him, but only on the conditions and all the Greek army turned home, for he doubted his power against his enemies in such strife.

Hecuba then sent to meet Achilles and told him King Priam's words about the matter of marriage.

When this news came to Achilles, he spoke for the army saying,

"Long has there been fighting against the Trojans, and it was time for them to see how much evil had been allotted because of a single woman, and how many thousands of good people had fallen, and it could not be known with whom the least of their property would be torn apart."

It seemed to him wiser to seek reconciliation so that all the good things in their land would not be wasted any longer due to this war. No attention was paid to his words, and no one wanted to end the strife that had long been ongoing and put everything else behind them.

They also did not want to turn away from it, neither did they want to make any beautiful agreements with the Trojans. It turned out that the truce was to be short-lived.

16

End of a Truce and Achilles Leaves the Fight

The truce-time, which was mentioned, ended when the battle-time came.

Palamedes led the Greek army with great effort into battle against the Trojans, and Delphebus, son of King Priam, led the army out of the city against the Greek forces, now gathering the forces with fierce battle and deadly combat, both were very eager, and there was now such a great loss of life that the bodies of dead men seemed to cover the entire earth.

Achilles did not want to go into battle with the Greeks, and none of his followers did, and they stayed at home in their quarters.

Of the rest, neither side needed to be urged to brave action, both were now eager for battle, especially the leaders of the army. Then Palamedes and Delphebus met and did not let their blows be long apart, both were fierce and skillful and had the greatest fighting spirit, they fought fiercely and Delphebus fell before Palamedes and many thousands on both sides.

Palamedes now encouraged his men in the attack and dealt the Trojans a triple blow in this storm. Sarpedon rushed against Palamedes and they fought fiercely until Sarpedon fell. Now Palamedes was glad because he had slain two of the greatest chiefs of the Trojans and he did not think there was any man who would be a match for him in a duel.

Alexander, son of King Priam, had become the greatest archer of all; he shot at Palamedes, hitting his neck and chest, which caused his fatal wounds, and he quickly changed from life to death, which just a short time ago he had not feared.

Trojans now pressed hard and put the Greeks to flight, and the Trojans pursued them all the way to their ships. They attacked the ships, and some set fire to them. The Greeks now ran to help the ships, while some defended against the attackers.

Achilles had great frustration with the sound of weapons when he saw the Greeks fleeing, but he did not want to help, so troubled was he because of the maiden Polyxena.

Among the Greeks, there was now no one as famous in his defense as Ajax, the son of Thelamon. If the whole day had been at hand, the Trojans would have won a beautiful victory, but night came, and darkness stopped the battle. The Trojans then went back to their city, and that night the Greeks mourned Palamedes for the nobility and kindness he had shown them.

That night, the oldest and wisest man called together all the chiefs of Greece and told them it was necessary to choose a king again and declared that it seemed to him that Agamemnon was the best candidate for that title if everyone agreed. He said that everything had been easier for them when he was king rather than after.

And he asked if there be one who would speak against it, but all agreed with motion, and Agamemnon was made king for the second time, and they all obeyed his command. The next day all Greece went before King Agamemnon and they all agreed on choosing him as the leader of the army.

A few days later the Greeks went to battle and the Trojans against them, and then Troilus, son of King Priam, was the leader of the Trojans. He killed many chiefs of the Greeks and that battle lasted for seven days altogether, and many fell and the Greeks struggled to resist, then King Agamemnon asked for a truce for two months, and then King Priam agreed to the truce.

At the set truce, King Agamemnon had a dignified funeral arranged for Palamedes, and both sides buried the bodies of their fallen men, and those who were wounded wept. During the truce, Agamemnon sent Njástor, Ulysses, and Diomedes, who were seers, to meet Achilles to ask him to join the battle with his companions, and when they came to meet him, they presented their case.

Njástor began to speak:

"Agamemnon, the chief of the entire Greek army, has sent us to you with this message, that he asks you to act as a good warrior should, and as a brave man as you are to go into battle with your friends and relatives, rather than lying in a military camp like a woman while other brave men go to battle and risk their lives.

"Many have fallen here since we came to this land, so that none of us want to let it be unholy, now do well, good warrior, do not let this misfortune be attributed to the one who has been the strongest of all the Greeks until this moment, and almost throughout the whole world his name is praised for the great deeds he has accomplished, so that the same time does not quickly take away his praise. When his fame has been so widely spread, and he loves the beauty of a woman so much that he forgets everything else that can bring honor, remove from yourself all this sorrow and grief and act according to the will of your friends."

But when they had put forward their plea, Achilles flatly refused to go into battle, and said that he thought it was great folly to continue fighting because of a woman and to lose many great leaders and brave warriors there.

"It is my advice," he said, "to make peace with the Trojans and have peace and respect from them afterward."

Now they told Agamemnon the king of his response, then he called all the commanders of the army to him, and discussed whether they thought it was advisable to heed Achilles' words or pay no attention to them.

But when he had talked about what he wanted, Menelaus, brother of King Agamemnon, asked that the battle should not be postponed even if Achilles would not come any closer.

"The Trojans have taken great power from us," he said, "and many heroes have fallen by the Trojans, and there is no one as powerful left in their ranks as Hector was."

Diomedes and Ulysses urged for peace and said that many of the bravest remained among the Trojans, saying that no one among the Trojans was stronger than Hector, and that this strife had lasted for a long time, but they did not know what would happen next, especially if they stayed there for a long time.

Then answered Calchas the soothsayer, "Let peace be made. Victory will be to the Trojans," said he, "if they go even so."

17

Troilus of Troy Duels Achilles

When the time of battle came, King Agamemnon led the Greek army.

Among them were Menelaus, Ajax, and Diomedes against the Trojans, it was the fiercest battle, and no one fought as bravely as Troilus of the Trojans. He inflicted severe wounds on Menelaus and killed a multitude of men, causing the Greeks to flee and ending their battle for the night.

The next day, Troilus and Alexander led the Trojans against the same Greeks as the previous day. Troilus then charged fiercely and injured Diomedes with a severe wound, and then he attacked where King Agamemnon was, and he did not stop his assault until he had wounded him, and then he killed a multitude of Greeks. And there was a fierce battle for several days, and many thousands fell from both sides.

Agamemnon said that the Greeks would not fare well in such a situation and asked for a truce of seven months, but it offered little to the Trojans that such a long truce be granted.

And King Priam then agreed to go for a while, and saw those who were wounded and weeping, and he made sure those who had fallen were buried.

While truces were set for them, King Agamemnon and Njástor found Achilles and asked him to join the battle with them when they came. But Achilles flatly refused his arrival and said he wanted to seek peace if possible, but eventually promised that his men should be in battle to support them.

King Agamemnon accepted that, and when the time for battle came, the Trojans went out of the city and the Greeks met them with outstretched hands. Achilles prepared his troops as carefully as possible and sent them to join the Greeks. The Trojans pressed hard against the Greeks, and most of all against Achilles' men who were called the Myrmidons, and then their troops began to flee.

Many Greeks were wounded by then, and countless had fallen, but Ajax, the son of Thelamon, stood so fast against them that no one could match him. After that, they fought for many days, and there was a great loss of life on both sides, and the Greeks suffered a great defeat and asked for a 30-day truce to bury the bodies of the dead men.

But when that time had passed, Agamemnon led all the Greeks to battle, and a terrible loss of life soon occurred in both camps, and the Trojans had never made a harder advance than they had to create Achilles' men's great grief, and they soon put them, the Myrmidons of Achilles, fleeing in terror.

When Achilles saw his men fleeing, he rose up fiercely and rode to battle with great enthusiasm. He called out, "Troilus meet me!"

Soon after he had entered the battle, Troilus wounded Achilles so that he was immediately incapacitated, and the battle went on for many days and Achilles was not in that battle.

On the seventh day Achilles urged his men to attack Troy fiercely and arranged them for battle and taught them tactics how they should fight in the battle. It is also important to tell about Troilus and the townspeople, that this morning he commanded the townspeople arm themselves and incited the troops, and ordered his men, saying:

"Remember the damage Achilles had done to us, and how many good warriors we had lost because of him, and the honor we have sacrificed for him, that we gain all the good and it may be difficult for us to forget. Even if we kill every person who has come here from Greece, it would still not avenge their war crimes that they have committed against us here or anywhere else.

"Achilles also remembers the recent unpleasant encounter and became incapacitated and has lain wounded ever since! Now it seems to me all the better if it were the will of the gods, that our kingdom will stand, that I and Achilles might meet in battle, and we should not both have great stories told that we should, and either I fall to him or my father would avenge his sons upon him."

Troilus now mounted his horse with all his weapons and rode out of the city first, ahead of everyone, followed by Menon and Aeneas and all their army, who are at this moment happy and cheerful, and encourage each other to advance and be courageous.

Achilles had now arranged his troops in one battle line, while King Agamemnon was with the Greek forces in the other battle line, and there Teopha advanced with King Agamemnon's banner. There was a great loss of life here with terrible provocation, and never had Troilus been as fierce as he was then; he rode forward in front of the Greek formation and struck with both hands, both men and horses, whoever was in his way.

He performed such heroism in his cause that all his enemies feared him. Some Greeks fled, and a large number of men had fallen. They had killed the horse under Troilus, and he was then on foot.

In this moment, Achilles came with his troops, and they both exchanged blows, inflicting many wounds on each other. Their encounter ended with Troilus falling with great courage.

Achilles wanted to drag his body to his quarters, but at that moment, Menon came down with his men. He had inflicted a great wound on Achilles. The situation continued until Achilles was exhausted and carried away.

He fled to his quarters, and all the Greeks fled as well. Menon had Troilus' body with him and brought it to the city, where he was greatly mourned by the Trojans.

For a few days, Menon led the Trojans out of the city, while Achilles opposed them. They fought for two more days, and Achilles was wounded by Menon both times.

On the third day, they met in battle, and Achilles was so fierce that he did not stop until he had slain Menon. All those men who had followed him fled, but he had a large force to support King Priam, and that entire force fought after Menon had fallen. They then closed their city gates again for shelter.

King Priam sent men to meet King Agamemnon to plead for a truce of 30 whole days, and he agreed. Achilles was healed of the wounds he had received in that time.

King Priam carefully prepared the body of Troilus and provided honorable burial to all the fallen chiefs, and they had good mourning and wept for many days. Hecuba, Queen of King Priam, became greatly angered at Achilles because he had caused the deaths of her two sons, Hector and Troilus.

18

Hecuba's Plot and the Fall of Achilles

Hecuba spoke to her son Alexander and asked that they both plot against Achilles for King Priam. She told him how much Achilles desired her sister Polyxena and the words that had passed between them. It seemed not unexpected that he would be swayed by his affection for her.

Alexander gladly accepted this offer; since he now willingly sacrificed his manhood for her advantage, he wanted to immediately deceive Achilles with pure treachery and the kind of cunning ploy he had previously employed well in battle or some other joint venture.

And on that same night, they secretly sent men to meet with Achilles, but King Priam was not aware of these betrayals. These men brought the message from Queen Hecuba that Achilles should meet her that same night in the palace's main hall if he truly desired to marry Polyxena as he had previously promised.

This was to take place outside the city; he was invited to attend this meeting where there was to be no disturbance or danger for all who came there. Achilles did not hesitate to attend this meeting because his love for her was so strong that it had clouded his judgment, and he was not wise enough to know the sacrifice it would be for him to achieve fame and success.

And that nobleman then carried out his treachery, as he went to the headland at the time he had decided, and with him was Anthilocus, the son of wise Njástor, and several more men, and they sought their shields outside but went into the headland unarmed, for they expected no attack.

Achilles had no weapon in the headland, except each of them had a sword in his hand. When they entered the headland, Alexander immediately gave them access with the party he had there.

When they realized the hostility and treachery of their enemies, they wrapped their cloaks around their left hands and swung blades with their right hands, killing many men.

Alexander now strongly urged on his men, and it is a great shame in his story that two unarmed men should stand against a multitude of attackers.

They now eagerly pressed forward, and in that sweep Anthilocus fell, but he had stood bravely, and had previously killed many men. When Achilles saw his fall, he let himself be carried to the place where it was best for them to defend themselves, and he trusted his fate to stand there.

At this place, he stood with his back to the wall, and he made sure that nothing could come from all sides to attack him. All his clothing was torn apart, and he was very wounded and tired from long defenses.

Achilles spoke to his enemies,

"Attack now vigorously, for it is a great honor for you to defeat me, a warrior as I am called. But I know that they will always side with capable men who have deceived me with such deceit and treachery, and if I had all my weapons here, you would have to pay dearly for my life, and I would serve many a man before I fell."

He then leapt forward and gripped his sword with both hands.

He now thought of nothing else but to kill as many as he could. He struck both hard and fast, and wanted to show his prowess and let it be seen before he was defeated. In this charge, he killed eight men, who stood so close to him with weapons that he could hardly move away or defend himself, and yet he dealt many deadly wounds and fell with a good reputation and great courage.

When Achilles fell, Alexander wanted to drag him away from the doors and give him to the birds, but his brother Helenus opposed it and found many reasons why it should not happen in any such way, and said that it was a poor revenge they had on his enemies and advised against this.

And when the Greeks learned of this news, they mourned his death greatly, then King Agamemnon sent wise Njástor to meet King Priam and asked if they could retrieve the bodies of Achilles and his son Anthilocus.

But Priam replied,

"Now it has come to pass that I answered for it when I asked for the body of my son Hector that there would come a time when we would not always wait together for this, but we will do this as long as a test of words has now occurred. And because you let me get the body of my son Hector when I asked for it and it seemed to me a great matter, I shall now not move away so that you do according to your loved ones as well as you like."

The Greeks then took the bodies of their men, and King Agamemnon had Achilles' funeral well prepared and greatly prepared for the funeral rites, according to the custom of honoring good men at the time.

19

The Arms of Achilles

After the fall of Achilles, King Agamemnon called an assembly and it weighed most heavily on who should take possession of the weapons that Achilles had owned, Ulysses the wise and Ajax Thelamonsson. A chair was set at the assembly and King Agamemnon sat there, and in his power was the armor that Achilles had owned.

People sat in a circle around the chair, the king asked his advisors what they thought about this matter, who should bear these weapons, as people claimed, until Neoptolemus, son of Achilles, himself arrived.

Ajax Thelamonsson stood up immediately and did not want to wait for other men's replies on this matter.

He walked in front of the king and spoke thus,

"Consider, noble warriors," he said, "what is being discussed here about the armor that Achilles has owned, whether Ulysses or I should bear it, or ask for it when Neoptolemus himself arrives. And it is most original in this matter that we both present our claim to the weapons, and look, noble warriors, whose sword is more broken or shield more struck, mailcoat torn, or helmet damaged, and if all my weapons are intact while his are broken, then I do not ask you to judge me for these weapons,

"But if it turns out that my armor is useless from the great blows of our enemies, and his protection unharmed and his sword little bent in hard steel helmets, or iron-rimmed shields, then you are not fair judges here unless you let the one who needs the weapons more and has better used their weapons bear them, may everyone know that the weapons will be invigorated by progress yet they will have little to do with it if they have been rented out for a long time; I expect you to say if I should bear them, that I should not be reluctant to refuse them. Now, as a just decision has bestowed on me the weapons and no one else, I like it very much that they be laid down on the hunting field, and let he who wants them take them."

But when he sat down, Ulysses rose and spoke up,

"It is a matter of little consideration that Ajax speaks of, for it can be quickly heard in his speech how much he cares about his courage and advancement, but he insults some people in his speech, and I will not speak against him, for he is brave in weapons and hard in action if he does not do it too arrogantly that he appears to be more arrogant than all brave men. It is not suspicious that his weapons are ruined, but I am not sure where they have been broken. It may be because his shield is very hacked that few have fought against him to defend it, and there may have been some equally responsible if he now leaves these weapons to his enemies.

"But where is Ajax as enthusiastic a man as Hector the brave, or Achilles the strong, or Troilus the strong? They all had the best weapons, but they were not as happy as they were brave, and therefore they did not last long in supporting their men. Now you may do with the weapons, both where they should be carried and in exchanging them. Let the wisest men now decide whether victory is likely to be won by the advancement of one man who is as strong as an elephant and strikes on both ends while he can stand, and he did not shield himself, nor did the wise man there who could advise many brave men, allow them to rush blindly into the enemy's weapons and fall before the spear."

After the other had finished speaking, it seemed to all that he should take up the challenge until Neoptolemus himself came to carry them out.

After Menelaus went to Cyprus to consult with King Agamemnon, he sent a man named Likomades to find Neoptolemus and inform him of his father's death. When he met him, he told him of his father's death and that Agamemnon had asked him to join his side with all the possessions he had inherited. Neoptolemus was shocked by the news.

He was not yet fully grown, but he was the bravest and strongest of men. He was a passionate man with a great sense of compassion, fearless in hunting and with a great spirit. He gathered to himself all the bravest men, and when he was ready, he went to meet King Agamemnon at Troy.

20

Ajax and Alexander

Next is to tell you what happened in Troy during Menelaus' time in Cyprus. When a sufficient amount of time had passed and the stones were placed, and the time of battle had come, Agamemnon led the Greek army to fight against the Trojans, while King Priam himself led his city's defenders along with his son Alexander.

They quickly engaged in fierce battle, and it was the hardest fight. Ajax was in the front line of the Greeks with so much bravery and fierceness that he threw his shield away, took his sword with both hands, and struck both men and horses with his sword.

Many people fell dead before him, and when he had advanced far into the Trojan army, he called out loudly and said,

"Where is now the seer, wise and advising Ulysses, favored leader of all the Greeks? Where are now those good weapons that you took after Achilles, and wanted them all for yourself? But I alone have been fighting today near-unarmed against my enemies, and your arrogance deprived me of such weapons. If I had them, I would not need any other man to protect me this day. Be as brave as you can be with your good armor and weapons, for there is more glory in fighting in the front lines than hiding in the rear, giving advice, or in undamaged equipment."

Both sides were fighting with great bravery and strength.

Alexander, son of King Priam, shot his bow all day and nearly every shot he made was fatal. He watched closely as Ajax killed many men, seeking revenge for his fallen comrades. Alexander shot an arrow at Ajax, which hit him in the right side between the ribs.

When Ajax realized who had shot him, he sought revenge and fought fiercely until he found Alexander. They fought for a while, both with great courage, until Alexander fell.

Ajax was so overcome with bloodlust and rage that he broke many bones and his spear in the fierce attack. When they carried him to his room to tend to his wounds, he was still raging and eventually died from his injuries. His men mourned him deeply and gave him a worthy funeral.

Alexander's body was carried from the battlefield with great sorrow, and King Priam had him buried with honor next to his brothers, Hector and Troilus.

Diomedes continued to fight fiercely, and he led the Greeks in their final push towards the city. He fought so hard that all the Trojans fled inside the city walls and locked the gates. Agamemnon ordered his men to stand guard throughout the night to prevent any Trojan escape attempts.

After Alexander's death, Helena was so overcome with grief that she wept for many days and her eyes became inflamed. She spoke of the difficult times that had befallen her and the many hardships she had endured. She said,

"Harder times are now over me, and I have received humiliation in many ways, and I cannot understand why our holy God would be so angry with one woman, and such hands the Fates have dealt me, all the joy has turned into such great sorrow and painful grief. I lost my father, my first land, my relatives, and all my kin, and was forced to come here to a better land with other people, which has caused great harm to many.

"Now, in addition, I have lost my most beloved kinsman, who wanted to make me worthy and respected with all his power and love, but that is my lord Alexander's undoing, and I will always be happy for having him."

She wept bitterly and these were her mourning words. King Priam and his queen Hecuba noticed her and they embraced her in every way possible, treating her as if she were their own daughter, and always having her by their side.

The next day after Alexander's fall, King Agamemnon marched with all his army to the city walls, and urged them to come out for battle, but King Priam did not come out and none of his men fought that day. They let the city stand and fortified with all its walls and stone castles, as much as they could, and they all waited patiently, relying on whatever provisions they had.

21

The Warrior Women of the North

At that time, while the Trojans remained within the walls, a woman named Penticelena came to the camp of King Priam with great sorrow. She was as strong and powerful as a five men and was adorned with weapons, and had great skill in war.

She was also very beautiful and courteous in all things. Many women were with her, they were fierce and tough. Such women were called shield-maidens in the Nordic countries.

When Priam saw the great strength and hospitality that he could have with this army, which had just come to him with such a desire for bloodshed, he went out of the city with all his troops to fight against King Agamemnon.

When both sides met, there were shield-maidens among the Trojan forces, and they formed a formation for King Priam's forces against the Greek forces.

The Trojans' weapons were the first to hit the Greeks, and there was great loss of life on both sides, but much more among the Greeks. The Greeks then saw no other solution but to retreat and run to their rooms, and they had lost many good men. It was now night time, and King Priam went back to the city with his army.

So, for several days, the Trojans stopped fighting and the Greeks were nearly defeated. They retreated to their camps, and many loved ones are still held captive; they set fire to the Greek ships and burned many of them, but the Greeks managed to save most of their people because they had both a large army and were well-defended.

Next came Neoptolemus, who was also called Pyrrhus, with a large army to join the Greeks, and they were very pleased with him, expecting that he would be as brave and successful as his father. When he arrived, he took the weapons that belonged to his father Achilles, but with great sorrow.

Now Agamemnon wanted to prepare for battle, and they sounded the trumpets and all the chiefs prepared for the fray, taking up their weapons. Neoptolemus took all his father's armor, which was so well made that hardly any other like it could be found anywhere in the world; and when he was dressed in this armor, he leapt onto his horse, full of courage and fury, like a snake full of venom.

He spoke these words before he rode out of the camp with great courage,

"It is true to say that it is a great shame for King Agamemnon and other chiefs of Greece to have come here with such a large army to besiege such a small fortress, that there are probably examples where an army of equal strength has come into one man's chambers, as has been gathered here. Many winters have been spent sitting around this city.

"We have lost all our best friends and relatives, and if I must count such things, then what I regret the most is if such a misfortune should spread to our kindred on either land, that one woman has caused the destruction of the great multitude of men who have come from Greece. And before one woman chases me from the battlefield, I will be as small as the lightest feather on the wind, and I would rather lie dead on the road than suffer such shame and disgrace."

King Priam now finished passing the city walls and rode out of the city with a large army armed for battle.

In this army was the fierce woman who was previously mentioned, and after a short time had passed, they met, Neoptolemus and the brave Penticelena, and they engaged with weapons, and although she was a woman, she did not run from him and fought all day until the night, and no man intervened in their duel, and neither had the upper hand on that day.

It is said that this battle lasted for several days with great loss of life, and on one day, Neoptolemus attacks this same woman, but she resists him so fiercely that no man would dare to intervene, as no other fate was more humiliating.

They fought until they were exhausted, and although it is said that she inflicted many great wounds on him, he finally overpowered her, though it was difficult for him. After that, there was a retreat among the Trojans, and Agamemnon pursued them with his army, Neoptolemus killing many men in the retreat.

22

Disunity in Troy

The Trojan men who escaped managed to evade the greatest threat at the city gates, and then Greeks encircled the city with their entire army, allowing no one to leave the gates.

The Greeks now attacked from all around the city, but they saw that they would suffer great losses before the city could be conquered, as there were still many brave men defending the city and its walls, and there was a large number of Trojan defenders. They had many great battle formations, and were already planning how to overcome their enemies. They had many courageous men to defend their city, but they were vastly outnumbered by the Greeks.

Now it is to be told that King Priam and his men were in talks with the city leaders. It seemed very narrow of options to them, considering what had happened. These Trojan chieftains went before King Priam: Antenor and Polidamas.

Antenor spoke and said that this situation seemed very difficult for them and that they might not hold out much longer unless they took some action that might be effective, or, alternatively, they should observe and wait until a better opportunity presented itself, perhaps at a cost.

After this warning, King Priam convened a meeting. When all the chieftains had gathered, he asked who should propose the best and most advisable course of action.

Antenor spoke first among them.

He said that it seemed to him that their situation was very difficult, because there had been such a long and fierce war between them and the Greeks. They had fought with them outside the city walls and had not been able to hold them off for long.

Now it seemed to him that their strength was failing and that their troops were badly damaged. Hector had fallen, along with many other great warriors who had no equal.

But there were still many of the strong warriors left in the Greek camp, including the brothers Agamemnon and Menelaus, Neoptolemus, Pyrrhus, Diomedes, and Ajax, as well as their wise counselors Njástor and Ulysses. Meanwhile, they were besieged and in danger inside the city walls. It did not seem to him that they had any alternative but to seek peace with the Greeks, with the condition that Helena be returned to them, and then to end the war and the bloodshed.

After he had spoken as he wished, Amphimacus, son of Priam, rose up.

He was young but strong, full of courage, and the most steadfast man in all his nature. He spoke to Antenor and all the other men who wanted to make peace.

"I say that those who want to ask for peace from their enemies rely more on hope than on good judgment. It is not becoming for men, especially leaders, to ask their enemies for peace, and to offer good things in exchange for evil. Those who do so are motivated by fear and weakness, and they become vulnerable to their enemies, who are like wolves.

"The only thing to do is to go out of the city with all our might and fight with the Greeks until one of two things happen: we achieve a glorious victory or we fall with honor. Either outcome is better than crawling under the beard of our enemies and being subject to their whims and insults, and honoring those who have done us the most harm."

Then Aeneas stood up. He was becoming an older man, and was very wise, the greatest strategist among the Trojans, and had been a great warrior and brave in battle.

He spoke briefly and said he thought in this way,

"A great storm has arisen from the journey of Alexander to Greece, to even take away Helena, the beautiful wife of Menelaus. It was also his intention to sail from here with such a large army from Phrygia as he himself desired, and to have with him the best warriors nearby of all the people in the country, so that he would avenge all the atrocities that the Greeks had committed here. But it seems to me that little achievement or reparation has been made for what was then done, for he did not kill any renowned warriors, rich lords, or governors of Greece.

"Rather, he pursued that purpose which is of little reparation to us and the Greeks. Now, as some of our men have thought, it would not be honorable to take Helena away from Greece, and for many men, that journey has become a long-lasting shame. We have now lost almost all of our best and bravest men, and it seems to me unlikely that we will regain the losses we have suffered from them.

"It appears to me that it would be wiser to make peace with them and have their friendship, if that can be possible, and accept their support if they will. We should not sacrifice more brave men and lose our wealth and freedom, and even our city, just to uphold Amphimacus' reputation and glory and wish to see the Greeks fall."

And when Aeneas had finished his speech, Elias Polydamas stood up and spoke,

"I would quickly and nobly express my desire that peace should be sought if I could decide, we have fought for too long because of one woman, and therefore endured hardship and discomfort, although eventually a truce would be made with the Greeks, where we can see that no truce or progress will come of it or any revenge from our hands for our men, such a force as we have to bear, even if our kinsmen are never avenged, those we have lost because we risked our lives, then our wives, children, and all our surviving relatives are in discomfort when we have fallen, and our enemies take the city by force, and then never again will discomfort and expulsion come from our effort if our dispute ends in this way."

After that, each of the other chieftains stands up, and they all wished for peace, but let it be borne in such a force, and everyone had spoken as they wished. Then King Priam raised his hand, he had been silent for a long time and listened to their deliberations, carefully weighing the advice of his counselors.

He then spoke angrily and complained with great rage,

"To those men I will entrust my case who should be called my advisors, and you have testified in your words that we have received such great damage and loss of men from the Greeks that we will never endure both. It will not escape my memory because you do not testify so often how much strife they have driven to us, first that they killed innocent Laomídón my father and besieged our city, then plundered but all our city's wealth and took away my own sister, and although first I was so grieved by the idea we were all obliged to take revenge, we first sought with the Greeks that they would send back

Eseone my sister and then peace would be made between us, rather than we sent from here to Greece, and Antenor went to seek, and no man will forget as brave and spirited are the words he received from those Greeks and came back so prepared that time

"He urged most of all, after meeting them, that we should attack the Greeks, he was also on that expedition with Alexander when Helena was taken away and he urged then most for war and violence, and this is the same Antenor who now wants to ask for mercy and seek reconciliation with gentleness with our enemies, he now finds it good to submit to their power and thus be under their mercy, whatever they want to inflict on us would be better if we beg for mercy or other reasons, they will call us all but conquered, we are still not badly positioned to fight as long as we have such a good stronghold as the city is.

"And I shall lose my life before I submit to tribute under the Greeks, and let that lie far from our family's honor, and I tell you that I shall never reconcile with the Greeks as long as I can sit on my horse, and bear my weapon. Be now all ready to go out of the city when I blow the war trumpet, and my horn will call the charge. I shall then end this battle that we have now with the Greeks, so that I shall gain victory and honor or fall with the other choice in honor and bravery."

After that, their conversation ended and they each went home to their households.

King Priam called his son Amphimacus for a private talk and said,

"I have great suspicion about those men who were most eager for peace today that they will be plotting some treacherous plans against us which we will not be able to respond to if progress is made if no peace is made with the Greeks according to their will. Now I have thought that I will summon them to my hall for a feast the next day when I have the greatest suspicion about this matter, I will pretend to take some counsel from them about our predicament, but I want you to come there with a large force of well-armed men and kill them all, so that they do not carry out any treachery even if they wish to."

Amphimacus praised this plan greatly, said he certainly knew that they would be plotting treachery, and promised to come at the appointed time, as was planned.

On that very day, the Trojan leaders held a secret meeting among themselves, the same ones who had earlier been involved in treachery with King Priam, including: Antenor, Polydamas, Engladon, Ampedamus, Pagusmalus, Andesen, and Aeneas, Priam's son-in-law and kinsman, and many other chieftains.

At this meeting, Antenor asks whether they should abandon King Priam to his fate, because he would not accept any man's advice or listen to their wisdom, and would rather die with all his people than make peace with the Greeks. They all knew how angry he was with those who tried to make peace with the Greeks and asked for guidance.

Antenor said that Priam was a brave man, but he did not see everything clearly and would treat them with suspicion in this matter. He told them that they should consider some plan and take action that might benefit them, and seek other means that could prove effective, not hesitating to try something new.

If it seemed to them that there was no way to send men to King Agamemnon to seek peace through negotiation, they would have to work towards giving up the city into their power and risking their own people's downfall, and thus save their own lives at that same time.

It seems to the elder chieftains not less likely as Antenor laid forth, although they also thought they had good reason to go by the ends that the shields were to follow by fateful decisions, when King Priam had promised them to leave the city for battle and let the winner prevail, it seemed to everyone better advice to seek another course that might be easier to follow.

They now bound this with strong agreements, and no one should openly break or reveal another's plan, but both of their plans were to send Polydamas discreetly to King Agamemnon's meeting and tell him where they had come to think they had to save their lives, and they would be ready to make that bargain with them, to give up their city to the Greeks for peace and their protection.

And when he came to King Agamemnon's meeting and told him his message as he was ordered, the king gathered his chieftains and counselors and asked to whom it seemed they should put their trust in what was offered, but most of them did not see beyond his mind and accepted with a warm heart what he presented and were very happy that there should be an end to the strife that had long persisted, with great loss of life, but those who were the greatest sages, Njástor and Ulysses, thought there was something to be seen in the matter and did not want to rush forward with a decision but carefully examine everything.

Neoptolemus trusted their words well and went before his chieftains with a plan, and in the end, it became firm and steadfast that they would send a man with Polydamas named Simon.

He went to meet Aeneas, Antenor, and Anchises, and wanted to know if everything was well settled by the Trojans regarding the peace agreement and renewed with them this matter which Polydamas had offered.

And when he came into the city and found Antenor and Aeneas and intimated to them the matters that had come from the hands of the townspeople, about the peace agreement, and they were to make true earth signs and marks at each time the city should be known, and which side should be closed before they came to the city. Amphimacus kept watch over the bodies at night, while guards did so during the day.

Simon returned the Greeks and told King Agamemnon that he had heard all the words from the mouths of the townspeople as before the four of them had come, and everything is now tightly bound discussed.

Polydamas explained how the entire army should be led to the city during the night, and it was said that a horse head would appear over the city gate, through which they should enter the city, and the horses had been prepared in three ways, so it stood before the city gate and in that condition they praised to be, on the same night to open the city gate and lead the Greeks in and provide support for them, and tell them where King Priam would be and all the other chieftains they wanted to kill.

When they had agreed on this with themselves, as they wanted it to be, Polydamas returned to the townspeople and told Aeneas and Antenor how their plan was intended.

23

King Priam's Last Feast

King Priam now sat in his great hall with all the chieftains whom he trusted would support him in virtue and loyalty throughout all decision-making, for they should rather willingly give their lives with courage than abandon their lord to their knowledge with evil adornments and secret treachery.

There arrived his knights and all his outlaws, his wild men, who wanted to show him the greatest loyalty and virtue, and they were all of one mind that each would sooner fall, one across the other, at the feet of their lord, than surrender the city into the hands of their enemies and thus betray their lord and beg for tears and mercy, not knowing what they might be granted.

And this was a widely known danger of courageous and capable men, who had little choice.

The king now provided a fine feast for all these people who had come to his hall, all through the night, and then each man slept where he had wanted, for King Priam and none of his men knew of the sudden war that was to come upon them, and it was a great sorrow that such a chieftain as King Priam, so venerable, could not have dealt with these treacheries and hardships that his subordinates had committed against him with deceitful cunning, which even he had established, where he saw two of them by his own understanding what they intended.

Again, it always proves true that one cannot avoid the fated nor overstep the doomed. Had the king lived a better night, he might have had more words in his counsel, but his envy and fate would have taken a different course regarding the deaths of men and other actions.

But now it was reported that the day had passed and the night was coming; the Greeks dressed for war and prepared themselves as best they could and went fully armed to the city slope, and there was no resistance, because as soon as they came to the city, some of the city dwellers opened it up and led the entire Greek army through the city slope.

They then went with great force and haste throughout the entire place until they arrived at King Priam's hall. But no one had a clue about this war that was now made by the collusion of the city dwellers, so there was no descent from these treacheries that were done to Agamemnon.

They now took all the doors of the hall so that none of those in the hall could escape. Some jumped up on the towers and walls of the hall with broken swords; it was now difficult for them to defend themselves against their enemies when they awoke to the noise and clashing of weapons in sleep and intoxication.

Some awoke to death itself, as swords and spears pierced them, and then the city dwellers leapt up with great courage and bravery, and they grabbed weapons, and many had a man before them when they fell.

No one among the Greeks was more relentless than Neoptolemus Pyrrhus; he first killed King Priam by the high seat and then one after another.

Now each fell dead in their bed and sheets. Neoptolemus had a large, broad axe and struck with both hands, one after another, and most would think that he must not be human as he went forward, covered in blood all night. The entire hall floor was flooded with blood, so much that the dead men's bellies were pressed out of the blood.

The Greeks went fully armed all night throughout the entire city and killed many people.

Amphimacus, son of Priam, had not been in the hall. He defended himself for a long time with a large group of men by a massive stone, causing the Greeks significant losses before he was attacked. Then he and all his men fell.

The Greeks plundered and killed people wherever they reached and could access until it could be called a massacre. Many sought escape to save their lives.

Hecuba encountered Aeneas as she fled from the hall. She asked him to hide Polyxena from their enemies, but he handed her over to a man named Archilaus, who provided her with help for a while. Meanwhile, Kassandra and Andromache hid themselves in the temple of Frigg.

24

10 years, 6 months, and 12 days

When all the Greeks had gathered after the killing of Troy in its sleep, every one of the remaining leaders of Greece were in that assembly.

Agamemnon stood up and began to speak,

"At the beginning of my speech," he said, "I want to thank the gods for the glorious victory we have achieved, and I also want to thank you, distinguished leaders and brave knights, along with all the common people who have filled our ranks for honor and respect, as well as for our own enhancement of honor.

"Next, I thank you for your excellent counsel, brave actions, and the great pride you have shown in me, as we have now overcome our enemy and they have fallen in a different way, and you have now achieved fame and distinction, valor, and bold actions, as well as great pride and honor. For this, I shall stand by your side in the face of the gods for your trials and dangers, and it is understood that I shall do everything in my power to honor you with what I have gained.

"You shall receive whatever you prefer, whether wealth or honors, cities or castles, or if you wish to settle here in Phrygia. I want to share everything with you as you all wish, and I want you to make the decision on how to handle and maintain peace with those who have surrendered the city and have submitted to our rule, or who shall be granted peace from those in the city and are not under our protection. I want everyone to contribute their thoughts, as I want to have the counsel of all of you."

Everyone agreed to grant peace to all those who were separated from them in the treaties. Peace was given to them all, and they gained all their possessions, free and unharmed, along with all their defenders.

Then Antenor asked King Agamemnon to let him speak the message that he thought was most important, and he was allowed to do so, saying,

"First, I want to say," he said, "as I am most obliged to, to thank you Greeks for the truce and peace that you have given us, and also say the gods have given you that power. Not long ago, we thought that no one would go from them to accept being our guardians because we saw you more powerful than all nations. Then we thought that we, innocent foreign leaders, needed to serve to buy or save our lives.

"Now you have overcome us with your bravery and strength, but it is an honorable path for you to give mercy to those who were previously victorious and now rely on your mercy. I also ask this for many who are more deserving and able to accept it, such as Theseus and Kassandra, who have always contributed well to your cause and always as their father be victorious and powerful, and made war, and asked him to release Helena without obligation, and did everything so that you would get Achilles' body and much other good, and therefore it is my wish that you would grant us what we ask, and with the advice of other leaders, I accept that you give the son, King Helenus, mercy."

When Helenus had obtained mercy, he asked for the sake of Andromache and Kassandra, saying,

"They were completely innocent, and they had always contributed well to your cause and always let their father be victorious and powerful, and made war, and asked him to release Helena without obligation, or those people who cannot be controlled by weapons, but it is an honor and nobility to grant mercy to those who are nearly overcome"

King Agamemnon now summoned a meeting with his men and asked what they should decide, or whether the favor asked for should be given, and everyone agreed that the favor should be given, and so it was done, and the Trojans all received goodness and beautiful freedom when the favor was given, and all their defense, but they thought it was a great change, and when they had all divided the spoils among themselves, then all of Troy was burned and shattered to the ground.

The Greeks burned and destroyed all of Troy.

After that, the Greeks greatly increased their sacrifices, and with great expense, they thanked the gods for the splendid victory they had obtained. When this was done, King Agamemnon wanted to return to Greece with all his forces, but when they were nearly ready to depart, a headwind arose against them, and they could not sail away.

The Greek people now suffered badly because they became very homesick. King Agamemnon asked what they thought was the best course of action regarding this headwind. The seer Calchas advised them to offer sacrifices to the infernal gods and call upon them for help, saying that this would work.

It is said that King Agamemnon sacrificed his daughter named Iphigenia.

While this delay occurred in their journey, Neoptolemus constantly searched for Polyxena and could not find her, but he believed that she had a hand in his father's death. He was very angry with her and asked King Agamemnon to provide men to search for her, but she was not found. King Agamemnon then called on Antenor and asked him to search for her until he found her, saying that it was dangerous for the Trojans, because peace would be lost if she was not found.

Antenor then found Aeneas, who had no longer trusted himself to stand by her, and she was then found in the custody of those four, and they led her to King Agamemnon. Many chieftains, with tears and beauty as if they were of Greek descent, asked for her and thought that she was a true, beautiful, courteous, and most royal daughter.

After that, she was led to King Agamemnon and asked him to do with her as he wished, and she would agree to it, but he led her to Neoptolemus, and he stood there with a bridal sword, which he had naked in his hand, and asked Agamemnon that she should weep, and he had nothing to say but to ask him for that.

Polyxena refused to plead for her life. Then she spoke and said,

"It is not fitting for me to beg of him who has done this to my family," she said. "Many have suffered greater harm than I have. If you spare my life, do it as a man, not out of pity, even if you want to stain my life like an unsuspecting woman, as this can only lead to something humane. For now I can no longer protect my father or relatives, but I would have not chosen life with your father even though you let me have this payment now. Nevertheless, most will think differently about how you avenge your father when you have brought about my death."

His anger did not stand up to her words, but rather he immediately cut her head off, and that act was greatly condemned by all well-to-do men.

King Agamemnon was very angry, and directed his anger towards Aeneas, blaming him for the death of Polyxena, and so he called upon his multitude of nobles and his fortified land and all his defense.

Now the ancient phraseology applies here so that the more powerful one now had to decide, he made his journey as quickly as possible because he distrusted the Greeks greatly, as he had the king's anger. It was now expected that he could not be settled there without any opposition since it was a great hardship to be in the councils of one's enemies, and that King Priam, a good lord, should have been put to death by the treachery of his own men's multitude.

Aeneas took the ship that Alexander had used for Greece and as soon as he was ready, he set sail and had with him 3,400 warriors and many other people.

Antenor stayed behind in the service of King Agamemnon with 2,500 warriors.

They all went together, Helenus son of King Priam and Queen Hecuba, Cassandra, and Andromache, to Beronéne with 1,200 men.

Then Menelaus received his wife, very sad, but he soon comforted her with his flatteries.

After that, Agamemnon left Troy with all his remaining forces and brought everything home to Greece, and the historian says that the Greeks besieged Troy for ten years, six months, and twelve days more.

880,000 Greeks fell, but 690,000 Trojans fell before the city was won, and after the city was won, 100,000 and 7,000 fell.

There the narrative ends of the war between the Greeks and the Trojans, following Hercules's sacking of the city years before, when Priam's father ruled.

10 years, 6 months, and 12 days it lasted.

Also by Jasper Owens

"Tales from the North" features a wide range of themes, characters, and settings, providing readers with a rich and diverse journey through the myths and legends of the region. The book reveals the profound wisdom and beauty found within these ancient narratives, inviting readers to connect with the cultural heritage and traditions of Northern Europe.

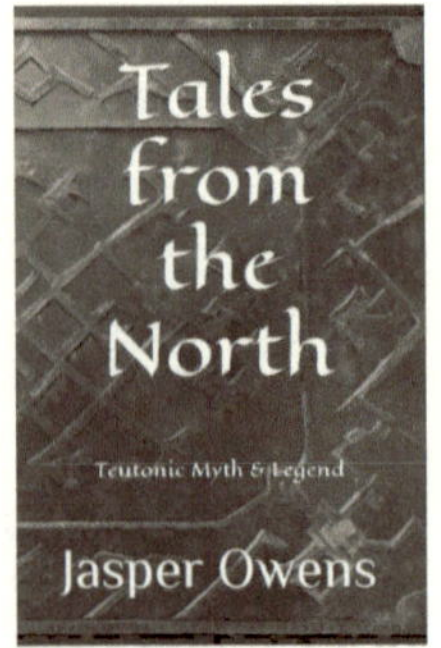

Tales from the North: Teutonic Myth & Legend
"Tales from the North" is a captivating exploration of Germanic mythology, with a primary focus on Norse legends. Featuring a rich tapestry of stories that have shaped and defined the culture and beliefs of Northern Europe. From the mighty gods of Asgard to the humble heroes of ancient sagas, this book brings to life the timeless tales that continue to resonate with readers today.

9 798223 388548